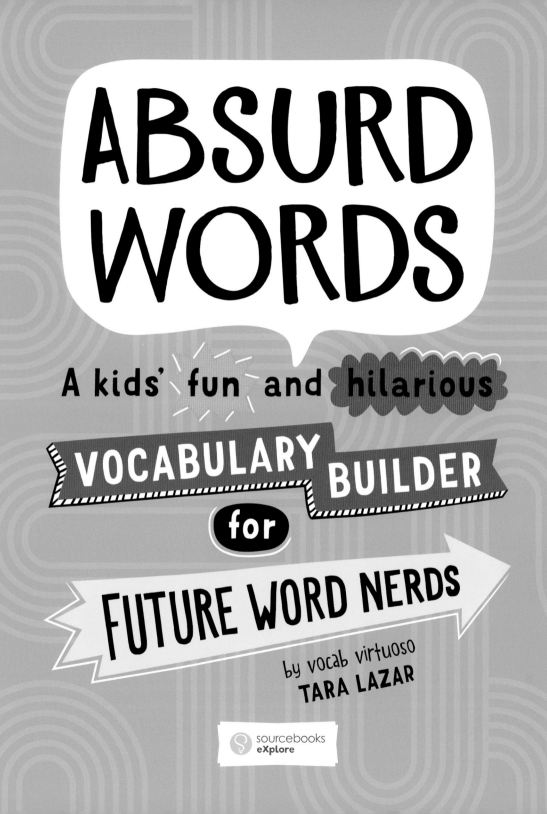

Published by Sourcebooks eXplore, an imprint of Sourcebooks Kids
P.O. Box 4410, Naperville, Illinois 60567-4410
(630) 961-3900
sourcebookskids.com

Library of Congress Cataloging-in-Publication Data is on file with the publisher.

Source of Production: 1010 Printing Asia Limited, Kwun Tong, Hong Kong, China
Date of Production: January 2023
Run Number: 5030656

Printed and bound in China.
OGP 10 9 8 7 6 5 4 3

WORD SQUADS

Groups of words that share something in common

INTRODUCTION

Words are amazing things! After all, without them you wouldn't be able to read this sentence. In fact, this whole book would be black and white scribbles that mean absolutely zero, zilch, nada.

So hooray for words!

And you know what makes words even cooler? There are *so many* of them—more than a million words in the English language alone! Plus, the Merriam-Webster dictionary *adds* about one thousand words to its pages every year. Some words are brand new. Others have been around for a while, but they have collected new meanings.

The number of words keeps growing as our lives shift and change. New inventions and experiences need new words to describe them!

But even though there are tons of words for us to speak and write, the average person uses only twenty thousand of them. Twenty thousand—that's it! That might sound like a lot, but it's only two percent of all available words they *could* use—such a tiny fraction!

Picture this: if the entire United States were covered with every word in American English, then the number of words an average person uses would only fill up South Dakota!

That means there's a lot of uncharted territory out there!

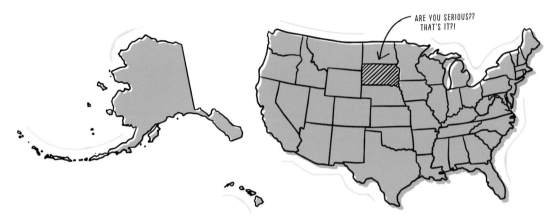

ARE YOU SERIOUS??
THAT'S IT?!

But why learn more words? Isn't twenty thousand plenty enough? Who cares if it's only two percent? People drink two percent milk, and they're perfectly happy with that!

But learning new words definitely matters. Because words equal power.

Knowing a wide range of words means you can always say exactly, precisely what you mean. You're feeling extremely happy, but "happy" just doesn't cut it—instead say you're *cock-a-hoop*! You're trying to describe that space between your eyebrows—you can now use one word instead of four with *glabella*. Want to describe something that is bigger than big? *Ginormous* will get your point across.

Words make stories more exciting. Some words are so overused, it's time to let them RIP—so instead of a pirate sailing the seven seas, move the boring words aside and create a *swashbuckler* exploring distant *archipelagos*. Instead of having your hero fight a plain old monster, let them battle a *basilisk* or a *firedrake*! Say goodbye to wimpy writing— watch it *vamoose*, watch it disappear! Become a master storyteller—a *raconteur*—able to captivate or *spellbind* any audience.

Words teach us about all the things we want to know about. If you're interested in space, you need to know out-of-this-world terms, like *exoplanets*, the word for planets so distant they are outside the solar system. If you play music, pick up new words like *hootenanny* to jazz up your language, and if you're into comedy, it's time to add in some *mirth*. Perhaps animals are your thing—this book has an entire collection, or *menagerie*, of real and imaginary creatures. You can be a superb meteorologist by learning rare weather terms. Whatever subject you to desire to know about, words can transform you into a wise and knowledgeable expert, a certifiable *guru*.

Again, words equal power. And the best thing about this book is that it gives **YOU** the power to have fun, explore, and learn at your own pace, on your own terms. The words have been organized into themes, so you can crack open to whatever section calls your name. And then feel free to come back again and again to keep the fun going!

There are heaps of ways to use these words, and by picking up this book and learning these wondrous and wacky words, you are sure to become instantly smarter, cooler, and more confident. These words are sure to captivate, amaze, shock, and thrill you. (And once you read this book, you'll be able to say that you were *flabbergasted*, *gobsmacked*, and left *catawampus* with *stupefaction* instead!)

So get ready to write them in essays and stories. Start texting them to friends. Slip them into answers the next time you raise your hand in class. Discuss them at dinner and stump the adults in your life. Learn outrageous word facts and share them far and wide. It's time to level up your language!

Each entry will look something like this:

word

(*pro-nun-ci-A-tion*), part(s) of speech
Definition(s).
Sample sentence that puts the word into use.
Synonym(s)

Parts of Speech Covered in This Book

- ► **Noun:** Person, place, thing, or idea.
- ► **Verb:** Action word! Get to doing it!
- ► **Adjective:** A word that makes nouns sound cooler.
- ► **Adverb:** A word that makes verbs sound cooler.
- ► **Interjection:** A word to interrupt or exclaim!

Reduplications

Some of the words are also what we call reduplications—words formed by repeating sounds. A lot of baby words are exact reduplications: *bye-bye, pee-pee, tum-tum, choo-choo*. But you can also alter the repeated word or sound to create a rhyming reduplication like *okey-dokey, bees-knees, eensy-weensy*, and *willy-nilly*. The most common way to form reduplications is by simply changing a vowel to create a new word: *wishy-washy, dingdong, crisscross, chitchat, singsong, flip-flop*.

Be on the lookout for reduplications throughout the book!

All throughout this book, you'll find funny cartoons illustrating some of the words, plus a bunch of extra mind-boggling details about others. You'll discover:

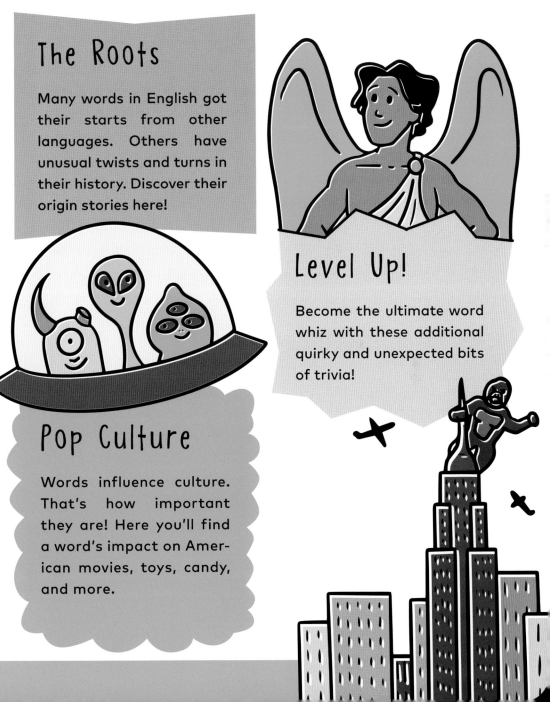

The Roots

Many words in English got their starts from other languages. Others have unusual twists and turns in their history. Discover their origin stories here!

Level Up!

Become the ultimate word whiz with these additional quirky and unexpected bits of trivia!

Pop Culture

Words influence culture. That's how important they are! Here you'll find a word's impact on American movies, toys, candy, and more.

A NOTE TO THE ADULTS

Research has proven that academic success—and life success—is tied to having a strong and varied vocabulary. This book introduces children to new words in an entertaining and engaging way, setting them up for a lifetime of achievement.

Each word in this book was chosen because of its WOW factor. There are words that are so much fun to say, or sound so unbelievable they don't seem like they can be real—all to encourage curiosity, and ultimately begin to quench it. The hope is that these words will inspire kids to have a love for language. Many of the words are actively being used in all types of literature today, and kids are sure to get excited when they stumble upon them and already know what they mean. And don't forget to have fun with these words yourself!

CLOUDLAND BUCOLIC

PAGODA ARCHIPELAGO

HOODOO VAGABOND

EUREKA COWABUNGA

LABYRINTH FJORD

GAZEBO BUNGALOW

BOONDOCKS JALOPY

ITCHY FEET

Words for journeys, adventures, and travels to new places

At the beginning of every school year, teachers seem to always want to know what you did over summer break. No matter what you did, make it sound like an epic adventure with just the right travel vocabulary. Make a visit to Grandma's more exciting by saying you *gallivanted to her bungalow in the willowwacks*. A quick weekend trip sounds a lot cooler when it's called a *sojourn*. Turn a ship into an *ironclad*, a car into a *jalopy*, and become a true *globe-trotter* as you discover new ways and places to tour!

archipelago
(*ahr-kuh-**PEL**-uh-goh*), noun
A large group of islands.
Hawaii isn't just one island—there are eight of
them, so the state is an archipelago.

boondocks
(***BOON**-doks*), noun
An area that is far, far, really far away. (Are we there yet?)
It takes nine hours to drive to Alfred's Aunt
Barbara's house in the boondocks.
Synonyms: hinterlands, willowwacks

bucolic
(*byoo-**KOL**-ik*), adjective
Connected to being out in the country—the lack of
complexity is often seen as beautiful and peaceful.
Let's take a horse ride in the rolling hills of the bucolic countryside.

bungalow

(***BUHNG**-guh-loh*), noun
A small, simple house or cottage.
Alfred bonked his head on the low ceiling at Aunt Barbara's bungalow.

catacombs
(***KAT**-uh-kohmz*), noun
Underground tunnels that are like mazes, twisting and turning this
way and that. Sometimes an underground cemetery or tomb.
The archaeologists searched the catacombs
beneath the ancient church for artifacts.

The Roots

There are many English words with Latin or German roots, but *bungalow* comes from the Hindi word *bangla*, which means "of Bengal," a region in India. One-story houses with straw roofs were common in Bengal. The British once ruled over India, so they used the term to describe the simple dwellings. Now *bungalow* can be used to describe any small house.

cloudland

(*KLOUD-land*), noun
The sky or a fantastical dreamland.
Penelope dreamt she could fly and live in a magical cloudland.

cowabunga

(*KOW-uh-BUHNG-guh*), interjection
A yell to express excitement and exhilaration.
Cowabunga! I conquered that ginormous wave!

Pop Culture

The word *cowabunga* became popular in the 1950s because it was the greeting in an old TV show called *Howdy Doody*. Later on, in the '60s, it was picked up by surfers who'd often call out "Cowabunga, dude!" as they hit the waves and had a good time. *Cowabunga* became even more popular in the late '80s, when the creators of the cartoon *Teenage Mutant Ninja Turtles* made it one of the catchphrases used specifically by Michelangelo, who was fun-loving and often spoke with surfer slang.

COWABUNGA!!!

The Roots

A *dirigible* is filled with gas that's lighter than air, like a helium balloon, so it can lift into the sky. But unlike a balloon that moves wherever the wind blows it, the dirigible was able to be steered. That's how it got its name—from the Latin *dirigere*, which means "to direct." *Dirigibles* were a popular mode of travel in the mid-1800s to early 1900s.

All airships are *dirigibles*, including blimps and zeppelins. The difference between a blimp and zeppelin is an inside frame. A blimp has no solid frame—if it deflates, it's just a pile of fabric on the floor. A zeppelin, named after the German man who invented it, has a solid frame inside to keep its shape.

dirigible

(*dih-RIH-juh-bull*), noun
Any airship, blimp, or aircraft that's lighter than air.
The dirigible flew over the football field to film the game.
Synonym: zeppelin

eureka

(*yoo-**REE**-kuh*), interjection
Something you say when you make an exciting discovery. You should say it right now because you discovered what *eureka* means!
Eureka! I discovered a new island!

fjord

(*fyohrd*), noun
A long, narrow, and deep inlet of the sea between steep cliffs.
Alfred wants to take a cruise to see (and maybe swim in) the icy fjords in mountainous Norway. All aboard!

foolhardy

(***FOOL**-hahr-dee*), adjective
Foolishly bold and adventurous.
People thought Thomas Edison was foolhardy in continuing to try and invent the lightbulb—especially after a thousand failed attempts— but he saw each attempt as a step closer to success!

The Roots

Eureka comes from an Ancient Greek word that means "I have found (it)." Legend has it that Archimedes, a scholar who lived from 287–212 BC, yelled the word after having a bath—and not because he found his rubber ducky!

Archimedes had been struggling to measure the volume of King Hiero II's crown because the king wanted to know if the crown was worth as much as its maker claimed. Archimedes needed to know the crown's volume to figure out its worth, but its irregular shape made it impossible to measure. But Archimedes had an epiphany while taking a bath one day. He noticed that when he got in the tub, the water would rise. His body displaced the water and added to the volume. If he were to submerge the crown in water, he could then measure its volume! He was so excited that he is said to have run through the streets of Syracuse, Sicily, still in his birthday suit.

gallivant

(*GAL-uh-vant*), verb

To wander around for enjoyment.

Every weekend, Penelope and her friends love gallivanting around the mall.

Synonym: roam

gangplank

(*GANG-plangk*), noun

A moveable plank or bridge for people to walk on—and off—a ship.

"Arrrrr, give me ye treasure or walk the gangplank!"
the pirate warned the ship's captain.

gangway

(*GANG-WEY*), noun

1. A temporary passage made out of planks of wood.
2. The opening people use to board a ship.
3. A clear passage through a crowd (generally used as an interjection to tell people to get out of your way).

The pirate yelled "Gangway!" as he passed through
the crowd to reach the gangway of his ship.

gazebo

(*guh-ZEE-boh*), noun

A covered porch, on its own and not attached to another building. Used for outdoor lounging.

Let's have our picnic in the gazebo, because it looks like it's going to rain.

globetrotter

(*GLOHB-trot-er*), noun

Someone who travels the world.

Nancy's neighbor is such a globetrotter that he is never home, so she's always babysitting his goldfish.

Pop Culture

The Harlem Globetrotters are a basketball team unlike any other. They show off fancy tricks and skills while playing, passing, and dribbling so fast it makes their opponents' heads spin. As the name hints, they have traveled all over the world performing their basketball *hijinks*.

The Roots

The first part of *gazebo* has the word *gaze*, which means to look. The "bo" part comes from a Latin construction meaning "something will happen in the future." Put the two together and *gazebo* means "I will gaze." A gazebo is for sitting outside, but it's supposed to have a great view too.

Just to make things confusing, the first recorded use of *gazebo* referred to a Chinese tower, so everything you just learned may be false, and *gazebo* may come from an Asian word instead.

No one really knows, so just enjoy the view!

hinterlands

(*HIN-ter-landz*), noun

A remote area where not many people live.

In February the mountains and forests of the hinterlands look like a winter wonderland.

Synonym: boondocks, willowwacks

hoodoo

(*HOO-doo*), noun or verb

1. *(noun)* A tall, unusually shaped spire of rock formed by erosion.
2. *(noun)* Bad luck.
3. *(verb)* To cause bad luck or misfortune.

Alfred wants to hike around the majestic red hoodoos of Bryce Canyon. Let's hope he doesn't break his leg, because that would be hoodoo!

ironclad

(*AHY-ern-klad*), noun or adjective

1. *(noun)* A large iron ship.
2. *(adj.)* Solid and unbreakable.

The Titanic was a majestic and ironclad vessel—so people were surprised when it hit an iceberg and sank. I guess it wasn't so ironclad after all!

The Roots

The second meaning of *ironclad* comes from the first. In the mid-nineteenth century, the warships that roamed the world were built with iron and steel instead of wood, making them stronger and better able to resist explosions and fire.

jalopy

(*juh-**LOP**-ee*), noun
An old, falling-apart automobile.
I'm not riding around in your rusty car—it's nothing but a sloppy jalopy!

junket

(*JUHNG-kit*), noun or verb
A tour taken for pleasure, to promote something, or to collect information.
The actor went on a junket around the U.S. to promote his new TV show about a junkyard.

The Roots

Sometimes words develop new meanings over the years...like *jalopy*. When the word first appeared in the 1920s, it was used to describe an old, rusty automobile. Fast-forward thirty years—to the 1950s—and people began saying *jalopy* to describe a hot rod, an old car revved up and transformed into a slick racecar. However, it's back to meaning a broken-down car that should probably be used for scraps.

labyrinth

(*LAB-uh-rinth*), noun
A maze of passages that is difficult to find your way through.
This corn maze is easy to get through, making it a corny labyrinth.

lagoon

(*luh-GOON*), noun

A small body of water near a larger body of water.

Penelope likes to sit on the shores of the lagoon and watch the moon's reflection in the still water.

Synonyms: pond, lake

landlubber

(*LAND-luhb-er*), noun

Someone who is uncomfortable or unfamiliar with traveling on any body of water.

Alfred really wanted to learn to sail, but as a landlubber he was too scared to even step on a boat.

Level Up!

Landlubber is not simply "land lover" mispronounced. The word "lubber" means a large, awkward, clumsy person—or a clumsy grasshopper, as a matter of fact. The Eastern Lubber Grasshopper of the Southeast United States walks and crawls more than it actually hops. (So why isn't it called a *grasscrawler*?)

pagoda

(*puh-GOH-duh*), noun

A Hindu or Buddhist sacred building that looks like a tower with multiple levels, with each level having its own roof.

In almost every major city, there are a pair of pagodas marking the entrance to Chinatown.

parapet

(*PAIR-uh-pet*), noun

A protective wall, usually along the edge of a castle roof or balcony.

The prince paced the parapet with his pet dragon, and he could view the whole kingdom while he pondered their next quest.

podunk

(*POH-duhngk*), noun

A tiny place or town that's rural, far away, and not easy to get to.

Aunt Barbara lives in a podunk town, and she has to drive hours to go to the mall or see a movie.

roundabout

(*ROUND-uh-bout*), adjective or noun

1. *(adj.)* a looping, circular path that does not go directly from Point A to Point B.
2. *(noun)* a traffic circle.

It's hard for Penelope to keep track of where they are going whenever her dad uses roundabout directions.

sojourn

(*SOH-jurn*), noun

A trip that lasts a short time.

We don't have a lot of time for a real vacation, so we'll just sojourn to the next town over for the weekend.

swashbuckler

(*SWAWSH-buhk-ler*), noun

A bold and bragging swordsman or adventurer.

The islanders admired the swashbuckler who refused to surrender to the menacing pirates.

The Roots

In the 1500s, the word *swash* meant to hit something violently and make a loud noise (think of *sword* and *clash* put together). *Buckler* was another word for a shield. Link those two words and you have someone who clashes around loudly with a shield!

wanderlust

(*WAHN-der-luhst*), noun

A strong feeling to want to travel and wander.

I could not deny my wanderlust, so I hiked across Europe and visited all the cities I longed to see, like Rome, Berlin, and Prague.

whirlybird

(*WUR-lee-burd*), noun

Another name for a helicopter.

A whirlybird can take you quickly from skyscraper to skyscraper in a city, because it can land on a roof instead of the airport.

willowwacks

(*WIL-oh-waks*), noun

A remote, wooded area without people living there.

Penelope wants to get away from the crowds with a vacation in the shady peace and quiet of the willowwacks. (I wonder if there'll be a lot of willow trees there.)

Synonyms: boondocks, hinterlands

vagabond

(*VAG-uh-bond*), noun

Someone who wanders and never settles in one place.

Vance was a vagabond who only stayed in a town for a week before packing up and moving on to a new one.

Synonyms: drifter, wanderer

zeppelin

(*ZEP-lin*), noun

A large German airship shaped like a cylinder. It had a rigid frame and was filled with gas to make it fly. Named after its designer and manufacturer Count von Zeppelin.

The zeppelin zigzagged on its slow flight and took a long time getting to its destination. No wonder the airplane won over travelers.

Synonym: dirigible

ziggurat

(*ZIG-uh-rat*), noun

A tower built of bricks, with a terrace around each level and a temple at the very top.

I climbed to the top of the ziggurat to see if the Earth is flat. (It's not.)

Pop Culture

In the 1960s and '70s, there was a popular rock band named Led Zeppelin (their hit "Stairway to Heaven" has been called the greatest rock 'n' roll song of all time). The band got their unusual name thanks to Keith Moon, the drummer for fellow rock band The Who. Moon recorded a song with future Led Zeppelin guitarist Jimmy Page, and they talked about forming their own band. But Moon thought the idea would "go over like a lead balloon," meaning it would fail miserably. He was joking, of course, but Jimmy Page remembered the *wisecrack* and used it a couple of years later to form Led Zeppelin.

TÊTE-À-TÊTE

GUMSHOE

CAHOOTS

CONTRABAND

INCOGNITO

SUBTERFUGE

ALIBI

CLANDESTINE

EAVESDROP

ENIGMA

WHODUNIT

RENDEZVOUS

CONUNDRUM

VERBOTEN

HEY, SHERLOCK!

Words used for mysteries, secret plans, and forbidden things

If you're a fan of a good mystery, you can now call it a *whodunit*. Or perhaps you are trying to figure out where your parents hid this year's Christmas presents—you can turn into a *gumshoe* and solve the *conundrum*. From disguises to detectives, spying and secrets, crimes and covert operations—you'll find everything you need to help you tell the perfect suspense thriller, be a better secret keeper, or simply have new words to describe your sneaky (or should we say *surreptitious*) sibling.

alibi

(**AL**-uh-bahy), noun

1. Evidence that a person was somewhere else when something (usually a crime) happened.
2. An excuse to explain where you were when something happened.

When his mom confronted him about eating all the cookies in the cookie jar, Alfred had an alibi to prove he hadn't been in the kitchen all day—so who actually ate the cookies remains a mystery.

cahoots

(*kuh-**HOOTS***), noun

A partnership, usually secret, with someone.

Alfred and Penelope are in cahoots to plan a surprise party.

The Roots

No one is sure where the word *cahoots* comes from, but the French word *cahute* means "cabin." Maybe when you're in cahoots with someone, you escape to a remote cabin to talk it over first?

clandestine

(*klan-**DES**-tin*), adjective

Private, secret.

Alfred hid the cookies in a clandestine place so his sisters wouldn't eat them all.

Synonym: surreptitious

contraband

(*KON-truh-band*), noun or adjective

(noun) Anything that is not allowed.

(adj.) Forbidden, illegal, or banned.

Candy is contraband in the classroom. (Unless your teacher is giving it out!)

Synonym: verboten

conundrum

(*kuh-NUHN-druhm*), noun

1. A mystery or a puzzle.
2. A riddle whose answer includes a play on words.

All the numbers have a conundrum to solve: Why is six afraid of seven? (Psst! It's because seven ate nine!)

Synonym: enigma

eavesdrop

(*EEVZ-drop*), verb

To listen to a private conversation without anyone knowing.

Alfred tried to eavesdrop on his parents, who were privately discussing what to get him for his birthday.

Synonym: spy

enigma

(*eh-NIG-muh*), noun

1. A puzzling person or situation.
2. A hidden meaning.

Alfred was an enigma to Penelope—was he her friend or her enemy? (Maybe he was a frenemy!)

Synonym: conundrum

Level Up!

Maybe you thought the word *eavesdrop* was really *ease-drop*. Easy mistake to make, since it **does** mean being able to *easily* drop in on someone else's conversation. (Well, as long as you don't get caught!)

But the word is *eaves*drop because it comes from architecture. The *eaves* are where an angled roof hangs over the outside walls of a building, and the *eavesdrop* is both the rainwater that drips off the roof and the spot on the ground where the water falls. If you stand on that spot under the eaves and look up, you will see a soffit, which bridges the gap between the walls and the roof, and has vent holes for air circulation. If you stand near an eavesdrop (ideally, not in the rain), sound comes out of the vent holes and you would be able to listen in on what's happening inside without anyone knowing!

The eavesdrop makes eavesdropping easy. So maybe *ease-drop does* make sense after all!

gumshoe

(*GUHM-shoo*), noun
Slang for a private detective.
The gumshoe got gum on his shoe and couldn't keep up with the robbery suspect.

The Roots

If you're following a suspect of a crime, it's important to be quiet so they don't hear you. Decades ago, detectives would wear rubber-soled shoes, or "gums," so they could be stealthy and silent in their pursuit.

The word *gumshoe* relates to the detective's footwear and has nothing to do with chewing gum—which makes sense, because gum can be pretty noisy if you smack it and blow bubbles!

incognito

(*in-kog-NEE-toh*), adverb or adjective or noun
Unrecognizable in some way; hiding your true identity.
Your bro wore a mustache to go to the dance incognito. (But you knew who he was!)
Synonym: anonymous

rendezvous

(*RAHN-duh-voo*), noun
1. A secret meeting.
2. A popular meeting place.
3. A meeting of spaceships in outer space.

There's a rendezvous at school tomorrow to surprise the basketball team and decorate the gym before the championship game.

subterfuge

(*SUHB-ter-fyooj*), noun
A deception, tactic, or device used to escape or avoid.
Alfred's fake footprints were subterfuge to fool Penelope and make her lose track of him.
Synonym: ruse

surreptitious

(*sur-uhp-TISH-uhs*), adjective

Sneaky and secretive.

I'm surreptitious when hiding my Halloween candy from my sweet-toothed sister.

Synonym: clandestine

tête-à-tête

(*TET-ah-TET*), noun

A private conversation between two people.

To make sure no one could hear them, the friends leaned close together so they could have a tête-à-tête.

whodunit

(*hoo-DUHN-it*), noun

A mystery that uncovers who committed a crime.

Did you see the whodunit movie? Can you tell me who did it?

The Roots

Tête is French for "head"—so *tête-à-tête* literally means "head-to-head."

Pop Culture

You probably know saying "Who done it?" isn't correct grammar. It *should* be "Who did it?" But, in the 1930s a writer invented this short, punchy word to spice up an otherwise average mystery book review. He fooled around with grammar and spelling to create *whodunit*—and *wouldntyouknowit*, the term stuck around.

verboten

(*ver-BOHT-n*), adjective

Strictly forbidden.

Going into the Forbidden Forest is absolutely verboten—hence the "Forbidden" in its name!

Synonym: banned

STEMWINDER VIRTUOSO

APLOMB WHEELHOUSE

WHIZBANG TOPNOTCH

GURU MASTERMIND

SOCKEROO BOFFO

NABOB WUNDERKIND

HOTSY-TOTSY BIGWIG

G.O.A.T.
(Greatest Of All Time)

Words related to being outstanding, number one, the best

What's something you know a whole lot about? That's your *bailiwick* or *wheelhouse*! Are you the number one student or ball player in your grade? Then call yourself a *crackerjack wunderkind*. And if everything is going exactly your way, you can now say it's all *hotsy-totsy*! It feels good to be successful, and we all like to be at the top of our game, so let these words help you prove your superiority in just the right way.

aficionado

(*uh-fish-ee-yuh-**NAH**-doh*), noun
An enthusiastic, extremely
knowledgeable fan of a
specific subject or activity.
*Penelope is an animation
aficionado and can answer
trivia questions about any
cartoon character or animated
movie quicker than lightning!*
Synonyms: enthusiast, buff

aplomb

(*uh-**PLOM***), noun
Cool confidence in a difficult situation, so
you breeze through the challenge.
Penelope passed her math exam with aplomb; she got an A+!
Synonym: sangfroid

bailiwick

(***BEY**-li-wik*), noun
A subject or thing you know a lot about.
*Alfred's bailiwick is video games—he owns every game system that
exists and knows all the secret and hidden tricks in their games.*
Synonyms: field, realm, wheelhouse

bellwether

(***BEL**-weth-er*), noun
A leader, either of people or things.
*The handbell choir is the bellwether of our annual holiday parade, and so
people always know when the parade is about to turn on their street.*

bigwig

(*BIHG-wihg*), noun
A person wearing a huge hairpiece. Wait, no...not exactly. A bigwig is an important person. (Although they *once* wore big wigs...)
Now that Penelope has won the Student Council election, she's a bigwig in school.
Synonym: nabob

boffo

(*BOF-oh*), adjective
Extremely successful.
The boy made a boffo dash to scoop up the basketball and score the winning basket.

connoisseur

(*kon-uh-SUR*), noun
A person who is knowledgeable enough to judge the best of the best in a specific category.
The candy connoisseur claims dark chocolate is superior in taste to milk chocolate.
Synonyms: expert, master

The Roots

The word *bigwig* really does come from important people who wore big wigs! Way back in the 1600s, King Louis XIV of France lost all his hair and decided to wear a large wig to hide his bald head. Other members of royalty followed the style that Louis set. Pretty soon, big wigs were worn by all the popular and wealthy people of France—after all, they were the only ones who could afford to buy the expensive accessories. The size of the wig began to represent the importance and wealth of the person wearing it. The bigger the wig, the greater your status in society.

crackerjack

(*KRAK-er-jak*), noun

1. A person who's incredibly talented at a certain skill.
2. Something that is exceptional and of high quality.

Penelope is a crackerjack softball catcher. She tags all the runners at home base!

guru

(*GOO-roo*), noun

An expert, teacher, or leader.

If you want to learn karate or martial arts, it is best to sit under the teaching of a guru.

Synonym: master

hotsy-totsy

(*HOT-see-TOT-see*), adjective

Good, perfect, exactly as you want it.

Goldilocks thought Baby Bear's porridge wasn't too hot or too cold—it was hotsy-totsy.

Pop Culture

The creators of candy-coated popcorn-and-peanut sensation Cracker Jack copyrighted the name in 1896, by splitting up the popular slang into two words. In 1910, the treat included coupons that people could collect and redeem for prizes. Just two years later, the company dropped the coupons and started slipping toys and trinkets into the package—instant prizes to attract more kid customers. There were miniature plastic airplanes, temporary tattoos, and tiny toy animals. Sometimes you'd get a small book of riddles or jokes. The toys worked their magic—Cracker Jack became one of the most popular snacks in America during the early to mid-1900s. It's even part of the song "Take Me Out to the Ball Game," which is the unofficial anthem of the Major League Baseball, sung during the seventh-inning stretch!

landslide

(**LAND**-slahyd), noun

1. When someone wins something by a large, or enormous, amount.
2. Rock, soil, and earth that tumbles down a steep slope.

*Almost everyone voted for Penelope in the Student Council
election, so she beat Alfred and Becky in a landslide.*

mastermind

(**MAS**-ter-mahynd), verb or noun

1. *(verb)* To plan and carry out a complicated activity or idea very well.
2. *(noun)* The person who plans the activity or idea.

*In the show Pinky and the Brain, the lab mice would spend
each day trying to mastermind how to take over the world!
But Brain was the real mastermind behind every plot.*

Synonym: genius

nabob

(**NEY**-bob), noun

A rich and powerful person.

Bob is a nabob because he gets the biggest allowance on the block.

Synonym: bigwig

pinnacle

(**PIN**-uh-kuhl), noun

The highest point, the peak. The best.

*The pinnacle of Penelope's year was getting to sing
and dance on stage with her favorite band!*

Synonyms: summit, apogee

sockeroo

(sok-uh-**ROO**), noun

A huge success.

The surprise party was a sockeroo—the birthday girl was truly surprised!

stemwinder

(*STEM-WAHYN-der*), noun
Something that is the best of its kind. Often used to describe an exceptional speech or the person giving it.

Penelope's stemwinder speech brought the house down—not only did her words leave the audience in tears, but they are still quoting her months later!

topnotch

(*TOP-NOCH*), adjective
Superior; earning a lot of praise.

I heard the talent show will be topnotch this year, so we better get our tickets early.

virtuoso

(*vur-choo-OH-soh*), noun
Someone who is really good at something. They make difficult stuff look easy. Often used to describe an extraordinary musician.

The violin virtuoso wowed the crowd with his performance of the very difficult piece of music, which he played with ease!

Synonyms: expert, master, whiz

The Roots

A stemwinder is a type of watch that was a new invention in the late 1800s. Before then, watches had to be wound by inserting a separate key. A stemwinder had a mechanism to wind the watch from its stem. This innovation was a marvel at the time, and stemwinder watches became known as the superior watch to own.

wheelhouse

(*WEEL-hous*), noun
1. A subject or thing you know a lot about. Or something you have a lot of skill in.
2. In baseball, the part of the strike zone where a batter can hit the baseball best (and usually get a home run).
3. The part of the ship that has the steering wheel, compass, and navigation equipment.

I can drive a car, a van, or a bus. But a house with wheels? Not in my wheelhouse.

Synonyms: field, realm, bailiwick

The Roots

The captain of a ship sits in the wheelhouse, where he can steer and check his direction, speed, and fuel. He has everything he needs within that space. The way we primarily use *wheelhouse* now works as a metaphor—it's your area of expertise, and you know (pretty much) everything you need to know about it.

This meaning didn't sail straight from the open seas but instead took a nine-inning detour through baseball. The batter's "wheelhouse" is the spot where he loves the ball to be pitched (right down the center of the plate and waist-high), where he can blast the ball out of the park. The wheelhouse is his sweet spot. And now that you know it, it's your sweet spot too.

whizbang
(*WIZ-bang*), adjective, noun, or onomatopoeia
1. *(adj.)* Something that is awesome and the best of its kind.
2. *(noun)* A fast-moving firecracker that goes... whiz-*BANG!*

On the Fourth of July, the fireworks that made smiley faces in the sky were absolutely whizbang!

wunderkind
(*VOON-dur-kint*), noun
A kid who is super-successful or super-smart.

The wunderkind won all the academic awards at school—even the prize for winning the most awards!
Synonyms: genius, prodigy, whiz kid

TURN IT UP

Words to describe cool rhythms, hip beats, and funky music makers

Have a favorite band, or play an instrument? Even if you think you lack musical talent, it's nice to have a few key words (Get it? *Key*?) to help you hit all the right notes when you want to talk about it. Like saying *crescendo* as the music gets louder or being able to describe the *staccato* sound of a drum. From types of music to different instruments, these are for anyone who appreciates good melodies, sweet harmonies, or making a racket.

bandwagon

(*BAND-wag-uhn*), noun

1. A wagon carrying musicians.
2. A popular cause, usually a political one.

When the parade's bandwagon passed by, the crowd was quick to "jump on the bandwagon" and sing along with the music.

cacophony

(*kuh-KOF-uh-nee*), noun

The clash and chaos of loud sounds.

Considering they never practiced, Penelope thought the school band would be a cacophony, but instead they played in perfect harmony.

Synonyms: discord, disharmony

calliope

(*kuh-LIE-uh-pee*), noun

A steam organ, named after the Greek muse of poetry.

Although they are similar, Penelope prefers playing the calliope instead of the piano.

The Roots

Circus showman Phineas T. Barnum was the first to use the word *bandwagon* in the mid-1800s. As his circus approached a new town, he would march a parade through the streets with a decorated wagon full of circus musicians. Townsfolk would follow the parade to the circus tents. His circuses became so popular that politicians running for office used Barnum's parade idea to create a buzz and draw their own crowds. People would literally "jump on the bandwagon"!

calypso

(*kuh-**LIP**-so*), noun

A style of folk music from the Caribbean, often with lyrics made up on the spot to poke fun at political people and events.

Calypso music played on the cruise to the Caribbean and had everyone on board jamming to its funky beat.

crescendo

(*kri-**SHEN**-doh*), noun

A steadily building loudness or force.

The concert got louder and louder with a crescendo until it concluded with a crash of cymbals.

didgeridoo

(*DIJ-uh-ree-doo*), noun

A long wooden instrument of the Australian Aborigines, which makes a low droning sound when blown.

If ever I visit Australia, I hope to learn how to play the didgeridoo, because I currently didgeridon't!

earworm

(*EER-wurm*), noun

A worm that lives in your ear. Eww—just kidding! It's a catchy melody—like the chorus of a pop song—that gets stuck in your head on repeat.

Help me, I can't stop humming that earworm! Sing another song to help me get this tune out of my head!

The Roots

OK, if you are easily grossed out, maybe skip this box.

Still reading? Don't say I didn't warn you!

Earworm is another word for an insect called an earwig. Hundreds of years ago, people thought this bug actually crawled into your ear and got stuck in it! (Good thing they were wrong.) Germans also had the word *Ohrwurm* for the same bug, but around 1950–1960 they began using it to mean a catchy tune that wiggles into your ear and stays there. And by the 1980s, Americans began using *earworm* the same way.

hemidemisemiquaver

(*hem-ee-dem-ee-**SEM**-ee-kwey-ver*), noun

In music, a super-quick note with the time value of 1/64th.

The note is so fast that "hemidemisemiquaver" takes longer to say than to play.

Level Up!

If you think a *hemidemisemiquaver* is fast, there's another note that lasts half as long, the quasihemidemisemiquaver, or a 1/128th note. And the *demisemihemidemisemiquaver* lasts half as long as that, at 1/256th of a beat! These speedy notes are typically used to add variety to slow sections in classical music.

hootenanny

(*HOOT-n-an-ee*), noun

An unplanned concert or practice session with folk singers and musicians.

When my dad and his brothers get together, one of them always pulls out a fiddle and starts a hootenanny. It's a lot of fun until my mom gets up to hoot along with the music. (Yep, she's embarrassing!)

maestro

(*MY-stroh*), noun

A musical conductor or teacher. Often used as a title of respect and admiration (with a capital M).

The maestro tapped his wand, raised his hands, and signaled for the musicians to ready their instruments.

mellifluous

(*muh-**LIF**-loo-uhs*), adjective

Sweet and smoothly flowing.

*Alfred relaxed during the mellifluous song
because it was so mellow and lovely.*

Synonym: harmonious

rim shot

(***RIM** shot*), noun

1. A *ba-dum-tss* drumbeat used to signal the humor
   of a joke—and it's usually corny humor!
2. A drumbeat where the tip of the drumstick
   hits the rim of the drum.

*As the class clown, Alfred wished he had a drummer to make
a rimshot after all his jokes, so kids knew when to laugh.*

staccato

(*stuh-**KAH**-toh*), adjective or adverb

1. In music, short, disconnected bursts of notes, like a drumbeat.
2. Abrupt or disjointed.

*Alfred taps out a staccato beat with his feet
when he spells "s-t-a-c-c-a-t-o."*

The Language of Music

If you learn—or already know how—to read sheet music, you'll find that English has borrowed many words from Italian as a way to provide instructions that indicate how a song should be performed. *Staccato*, for instance, comes from the Italian verb *staccare*, which means "to detach"—indicating that the music notes should sound detached from one another. Here are a few other Italian words that help us read music:

Adagio – slow

Allegro – cheerful or lively

Coda – the end

Crescendo – to become more (play increasingly louder)

Diminuendo – to become less (play increasingly softer)

Forte – loud

Fortissimo – very loud

tintinnabulation

(*tin-ti-nab-yuh-LAY-shuhn*), noun
The sound of bells ringing.
The tintinnabulation of the church bells echoed through the hills of the town.

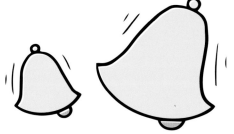

The Roots

Tintinnabulation comes from the Latin verb *tintinnare*, which means "to ring or jingle." It's onomatopoeia, similar to using *ting* or *tinkle* for a bell's sound. And when you have ringing in your ear, it's called "tinnitus."

vuvuzela

(*voo-voo-ZAYL-uh*), noun

A long horn that makes a low, moaning sound. Typically used by fans at soccer games.

The fans at the World Cup blew loud vuvuzelas and became a viral sensation because the sound was so strange!

Level Up!

The word *zydeco* came about when part of a French phrase was said with a heavy Louisiana Cajun accent. The phrase was *"les haricots ne sont pas salés"* or "the green beans aren't salty." If you hear a Cajun saying *"les haricot"* it does sound like "zy-de-co!" (In French, *les* has a "z" sound, the "h" of *haricot* is silent, and the end of *haricot* has a long "o" vowel sound.)

But wait, what do vegetables have to do with music? Cajun *zydeco* has rhythm and blues roots, and when someone has "the blues," it means they're down on their luck. "The green beans aren't salty" was used to mean that someone didn't have enough money to even put salt on their vegetables—and that means they probably had the blues.

zydeco

(*ZY-dih-koh*), noun

A type of Cajun dance music, usually featuring an accordion.

When people in New Orleans hear the quick tempo of zydeco, their feet can't help but dance to the rhythm.

zzxjoanw

(*shaw* or *ziks-JO-an*), noun

1. A Maori drum.
2. A fife (small flute played in military bands).
3. The musical conclusion.

Alfred waited for the zzxjoanw cue before pounding the drums at the end of the concert.

The Roots

A new word can get added to the dictionary if people use the word often enough (but it will be called a "ghost word" or might say "non-standard" in the definition to alert you that it's been made up). When *zzxjoanw* landed in the dictionary, it wasn't because it was so popular, but because author Rupert Hughes included it in his 1903 book, *The Musical Guide*. He thought others would know that it was an obvious hoax, but people thought it was legit! They knew Mr. Hughes as a musical expert, so he must be correct. For over fifty years, *zzxjoanw* appeared in Hughes's book through reprints and republications, and eventually got picked up in dictionaries too. No one ever seriously questioned *zzxjoanw* until seventy years after its first appearance. That's a long life for a word that doesn't really exist! (But it continues to live on in stories like this.)

LOLLAPALOOZA

COTILLION   HIJINKS

MASQUERADE

SHEBANG   HOOPLA

HULLABALOO

SHINDIG   JUBILEE

JAMBOREE

IT'S LIT!

Words for fabulously fun parties and festive get-togethers

These words are ready to party! Birthday party, graduation party, pool party. Instead of repeating party like a broken record, you can now use *jubilee*, *shebang*, *hullabaloo*! Having a good time with family and friends means there's a good chance it's going to turn into a *hoopla* full of *hijinks*! Don't all these words make celebrating sound so much more fun?!

convivial

(*kuhn-**VIV**-ee-uhl*), adjective
Festive, friendly, and fun.
Generally used to describe a
party with good food, drink,
or company. It can also be
used to describe a person
who is the life of the party.
*Sam throws the best parties—
there's good food, lots of
laughter, and the whole
vibe is always convivial.*

The Roots

Convivial came into use in
the mid-seventeenth cen-
tury from the Latin word
convivialis or *convivium*,
which meant "feast." It is
a combination of the prefix
con- (with) and *vivere* (live).
A good feast is sure to be
full of life!

cotillion

(*ko-**TIL**-yen*), noun
1. A formal ball or dance.
2. A type of ballroom dance.

*Cinderella made it to the prince's cotillion, just in
time to dance with him until midnight.*

fete (or fête)

(*feyt* or *fet*), noun
An elaborate party or festival; often held outdoors.
*Every year, the school throws the graduating class a fete with all types
of entertainers, lots of games, and chances to win really great prizes.*

hijinks

(*HY-jingks*), noun
An awesome good time.
*There are sure to be hijinks at Penelope's birthday
party because it's at the trampoline park!*

hoopla

(*HOOP-lah*), noun

1. Incredible excitement and commotion.
2. Exaggerated excitement or hype.

On New Year's Eve there's a lot of hoopla—fancy parties, the ball drop in Times Square, and bands performing all over the world!

The Roots

Hoopla comes from a French interjection, *"houp-là!"* (which is where we get the word *hoop* and the "hoop" part of hula-hoop too). *"Houp-là"* is like our "upsy-daisy," something a mother might say when lifting her baby out of a crib or highchair. Not wanting that sudden motion to make the baby fuss and fear, the parent says *"houp-là!"* to pretend it's fun and exciting.

hullabaloo

(*HUHL-uh-buh-loo*), noun

A noisy gathering making a great fuss about something.

What a hullabaloo for the hometown team's first championship—a parade, a party, and the mayor gave the players the key to the city!

jamboree

(*jam-buh-REE*), noun

A large, noisy, fun gathering.

On the last night of summer camp, we always have a bonfire jamboree.

jubilee

(*JOO-buh-lee*), noun

1. An anniversary celebration.
2. Any festival or joyous celebration.

My hometown is throwing a parade for its 150th jubilee.

lollapalooza

(*lol-uh-puh-LOO-zuh*), noun

An incredible, fabulous, awesome thing. Often used to describe festivals or large gatherings.

Alfred had the best day of his life at the new amusement park, so he started calling it an amusement lollapalooza instead!

masquerade

(*mas-kuh-RAID*), noun

1. A party with guests in elaborate, fancy costumes or disguises, usually featuring a mask.
2. A costume worn at this type of party.
3. A falsehood or deception.

Alfred came dressed as a mummy to Penelope's masquerade party.

Synonym: disguise

Pop Culture

The word *lollapalooza* had been around for decades, but in the 1930s cartoonist Rube Goldberg created a character named "Lala Palooza," helping the word become more popular. In 1991, Lollapalooza became the proper name for a touring music festival, once again boosting the word's celebrity. Except for a brief break from 1997 to 2003 and in 2020, Lollapalooza happens every summer, although it is now held in Chicago for four days and no longer travels.

shebang

(*shuh-BANG*), noun

A party or activity or place or thing. Often used with "whole," as in "the whole shebang."

Penelope organized the whole shebang for the animal shelter and raised enough money to buy kennels for a dozen more dogs.

shindig

(**SHIN**-dig), noun

A large party, dance, or other get-together.

The shindig at my friend's house on Friday will have a karaoke contest.

soiree (or soirée)

(*swah-**RAY***), noun

An evening party or reception.

After the science fair, the science club is invited to our house for a science-themed soiree.

The Roots

The French word *soir* means "evening" or "night"—specifically the time of day right after sunset. When the French used *soirée*, they were referring to activities done in the evening time. The English borrowed the word to use as a fancy version of *party*. In English, we generally spell *soiree* without the accent (although you're welcome to use it if you want).

Pop Culture

In the early 1960s, folk music topped the music charts. A popular TV show called *Hootenanny* featured bands playing pop-folk with a live audience of teenagers clapping and singing along. But in 1964, the Beatles, a rock band from England, began the "British Invasion," and folk music flopped as music from the Beatles, the Rolling Stones, and similar bands skyrocketed in popularity. *Hootenanny* was canceled, but quickly replaced by *Shindig!*, which featured famous rock 'n' roll acts (including the Beatles). *Shindig!* became so popular, another network started a rival music show called *Hullaballo*.

PANTALOONS GEWGAW

DOODAD AVANT-GARDE

MUUMUU POTPOURRI

BIJOU KNICKKNACK

VELVETEEN BAUBLE

BESPOKE CANDELABRA

FINNIMBRUN FESTOON

STYLE PROFILE

Words to brighten, spice up, and transform any look

Planning what to wear for Halloween or the next school dance? Better make sure you have all the right pieces, or rather *accoutrements*, to complete your look. To decorate your room, you might put up posters and things—some *knickknacks*, some *tchotchkes*, a random *doodad*. And to add a wow factor to things, you'll need some *frippery* and *foofaraw*. Whatever your style, let it be known with these words.

accoutrements

(*uh-**KOO**-truh-muhnts*), noun

Clothing, accessories, and other things required for a specific activity.

A medieval knight's swords, shields, and armor are crucial accoutrements for an authentic Renaissance Fair.

Synonyms: gear, equipment, paraphernalia

avant-garde

(*ah-vahnt-**GAHRD***), adjective or noun

1. (*adj.*) Unusual, daring, and experimental—
   particularly with art or fashion.
2. (*noun*) A group of artists, musicians, or writers or those from
   another creative field whose work is unusual and experimental.

The designers always create some of the strangest designs and most inventive outfits when challenged to make something avant-garde.

balaclava

(*bal-uh-**KLAH**-vuh*), noun

A warm, tight-fitting hat that covers the entire
head and face except the eyes and mouth.

No one knows who built that awesome snowman, because the kid who made it was wearing a balaclava.

bijou

(*BEE-zhu*), adjective or noun
A small and dainty jewel, piece
of jewelry, or decorative piece.
Its craftsmanship usually
makes it really special.
*Penelope's brilliant bijou
bracelet once belonged
to her grandmother.*

bauble

(*BAW-buhl*), noun
A small, cheap piece of
jewelry, trinket, ornament.
Tends to be somewhat showy
and the owner thinks it's
attractive—even though
others think it's pretty ugly.
*Aunt Barbara loves to accessorize
her outfits with baubles she
collects from her travels—it's
clear none of them cost a lot of
money, but she loves them!*
Synonyms: bric-a-brac,
finnimbrun, gewgaw, gimcrack,
knickknack, tchotchke, trinket

The Roots

Bijou comes from the
Breton word *bizou*, which
meant "ring." The origin
alone makes *bijou* a rare
jewel in the English lan-
guage, because the first
English speakers had
little contact with Breton
people, and therefore our
language borrowed very
few words from them!

bespoke

(*buh-SPOHK*), adjective
Anything made especially
to suit you.
*Because her mom was really
good at making things, Penelope
always had a bespoke Halloween
costume that was one of a kind!*
Synonym: custom-made

boondoggle

(*BOON-daw-guhl*), noun

1. A braided cord used as a hatband, ornament, or slide for a neckerchiefs.
2. An activity that is wasteful or doesn't make a lot of sense to spend time and money on.

Alfred and Penelope made boondoggles out of yarn and plastic at camp—Penelope used hers for a bracelet, and Alfred made his into a keychain.

candelabra

(*kan-dl-AH-bruh*), noun

A fancy candle holder with multiple branches.

Carry the candelabra carefully so you don't make the candles topple!

The Roots

Boy Scouts at summer camp in the late 1920s braided plastic and leather cords into lanyards, and they called their craft a *boondoggle*. During the Great Depression a few years later, when many Americans were out of work, the government set up a special division to teach people new skills. Teachers were shown how to make *boondoggles* so they could teach children in poor neighborhoods how to reuse materials for crafting. However, many people saw this is as waste of time and government resources. The "waste" meaning of *boondoggle* stuck around, and now we just call a lanyard...a lanyard!

diaphanous

(*dahy-AF-uh-nuhs*), adjective

Something light and sheer you can see through.

The outlines of the ballerina's legs are visible through her diaphanous *skirt.*

Synonym: gossamer

doodad

(*DOO-dad*), noun

1.   A small, pretty object used to decorate.
2.   A gadget or tool whose name you have forgotten.

Penelope's necklace has a little doodad *hanging from it that everyone admires.*

Synonyms: doohickey, thingamabob, thingamajig, whatchamacallit, whatsis

festoon

(*fe-STOON*), noun or verb

1.   (*noun*) A chain or garland of ribbons or flowers.
2.   (*verb*) To decorate in a festive fashion.

Alfred festooned *the party room with a* festoon *of flowers.*

finnimbrun

(*FIN-im-bruhn*), noun

A little decorative item.

I'm glad Alfred brought a new finnimbrun *for my collection of miniature one-flower vases.*

Synonyms: bauble, bric-a-brac, gewgaw, gimcrack, knickknack, tchotchke, trinket

foofaraw

(*FOO-fuh-raw*), noun

1. Outrageous, over-the-top decorations.
2. A fuss over something not worth fussing about.

For Christmas, Penelope's family puts up four trees, has lots of yard decorations, and adds lights to everything. The whole neighborhood is beautiful, but theirs looks like a lot of foofaraw.

frippery

(*FRIP-uh-ree*), noun

1. Clothes that are so overly fancy that it's ridiculous.
2. Anything that is unnecessarily showy and over-the-top.

Penelope's mom offered her frippery from the eighties for the dance, but Penelope didn't want to be seen wearing so many ruffles!

froufrou

(*FROO-froo*), noun

Decorations or accessories that are overly frilly, lacy, or ruffly.

Fifi the French poodle is always dressed in pink bows and a tutu—how froufrou!

Synonym: chichi

gewgaw

(**GOO**-*gaw*), noun

Any small thing that looks fancy, but it is actually worthless.

When I'm at the mall, I stare into store windows, amazed by all the sparkly bling inside, but my mom tells me to keep moving—they're just gewgaws.

Synonyms: bauble, bric-a-brac, gimcrack, knickknack, tchotchke, trinket

gimcrack

(**JIM**-*krak*), noun

A fancy item that is completely useless.

My friends spend their allowance on silly decorations for their rooms, but I'm saving my money, not spending it on gimcracks!

Synonyms: bauble, bric-a-brac, gewgaw, knickknack, tchotchke, trinket

gossamer

(**GOS**-*uh-mer*), noun

Any thin, delicate, light material.

A butterfly's wings are made of gossamer *fibers— even the slightest touch can damage them.*

Synonym: diaphanous

grotesque

(*groh-***TESK**), adjective or noun

1. *(noun)* A style of art that uses fantastical human or animal shapes that look bizarre, unusual, or comical in shape or figure.
2. *(adj.)* Bizarre, unusual, or comically ugly in shape or form.

The ancient Romans loved painting grotesque *art on their walls—the humans and animals are so weird, it's unknown why they liked the style of art.*

knickknack

(*NIK-nak*), noun
A little something of little value, usually used to decorate something.
Rebecca's backpack is covered with all sorts of knickknacks—cheesy key chains, silly patches, and cheap pins and buttons.
Synonyms: bauble, bric-a-brac, gewgaw, gimcrack, tchotchke, trinket

muumuu

(*MOO-moo*), noun
An oversized, shapeless dress with bright patterns, worn by Hawaiian women but sometimes worn as a dress around the house.
My mom wears a muumuu when she's relaxing around the house, and I wear my pajamas.

The Roots

If you have a "knack" for something—like soccer or the violin—it means you have the skill for it. It's possible the word came from the German *knacken*, which means "to solve a puzzle." The poet and author Chaucer introduced a different meaning for "knack" in *The Canterbury Tales*: a sneaky trick. A sneaky trick, while dishonest, is also clever. The "clever" connotation of *knack* stuck around and eventually was used to refer to objects that had a flair of genius to them. "Knick-knack" appeared in the 1700s by reduplicating "knack," and the new word meant "a trinket." Maybe people at the time thought trinkets were clever, because they were so popular, you could visit a *knick-knackatory* (a store that sells knickknacks) to buy one from a *knick-knackatorian* (a person who sells them)!

pantaloons
(*pan-tuh-LOONZ*), noun

The name for men's pants or trousers a few hundred years ago.

You might look silly wearing pantaloons *now because they are way out of style.*

potpourri
(*poh-poo-REE*), noun

1. A mix of dried flowers and spices that smells nice, used as a room freshener.
2. A mix of anything, usually things that aren't related.

My mom put a potpourri *of dried rose petals, lavender, and orange rind in the bathroom, and boy, does that stuff stink!*

Synonyms: hodgepodge, gallimaufry, mishmash

tchotchke
(*CHAHCH-kee*), noun

An inexpensive little decorative thing.

Whenever she has a little bit of money, Penelope buys a tchotchke—*she likes to line them up on her windowsill and dresser.*

Synonyms: bauble, bric-a-brac, gewgaw, gimcrack, knickknack, trinket

velveteen
(*vel-vi-TEEN*), noun

A soft, smooth cotton fabric that imitates velvet.

I like to cuddle with my velveteen *stuffed animal—she's so comfy and cozy.*

RIPSNORTER

HUZZAH

HOOEY

RAZZMATAZZ

GADZOOKS

QUIDDITY

CHICHI

ISHKABIBBLE

OUTLANDISH

SPIFFY

PANACHE

SCINTILLATING

JUGGERNAUT

PIZZAZZ

HEAD TURNERS

Words for anything or anyone that distinctly stands out and is impossible to ignore

The latest game or toy has everyone *spellbound*—they just can't turn their eyes away. If you're trying to make a good impression, you need a *humdinger* or something *flamboyant*— something cool or bold—to make you stand out. Sometimes things are just so wonderful (*splendiferous*), or so extra (*superfluous*), it just stops you in your tracks. Or maybe it's a feeling you can't ignore—like the fear of being phone-less or the need to get something done? Yup—there are words to describe those too.

anomaly

(*uh-**NOM**-uh-lee*), noun

Something that is out of the ordinary—not normal or expected.

A frog with five legs is an anomaly—it must be a science experiment gone wrong.

behoove

(*bih-**HOOV***), verb

To feel you MUST do something, either for your benefit or someone else's.

Alfred feels behooved to help old ladies cross the street—even if he's in a hurry!

chichi

(***SHEE**-shee*), adjective or noun

When someone or something is overly fancy, fussy, or decorative in style.

She called that Chihuahua with the diamond collar a chichi doggie.

Synonym: froufrou

The Roots

Have you heard of the French word *chic*, which means something fashionable and elegant? Well, *chichi* comes from *chic*—but it generally means that what was chic has gone *way* over the top!

doppelgänger

(*DOP-uhl-gang-er*), noun
Someone who looks a lot like someone else; almost like they're twins—except they aren't.

I did a double take when I thought I saw Dad, but it was just his doppelgänger.

The Roots

Doppelgänger comes from the German words *doppel* (double) and *gänger* (walker or goer). It was believed that you could have a twin ghost, and the idea of a doppelgänger became a common theme in horror stories. The scary meaning has slowly faded (just like a ghost!), and today *doppelgänger* is generally just used to refer to anyone who looks exactly like someone else.

effervescence

(*ef-er-VES-ens*), noun
1. When a person or event is bubbly, lively, and exciting.
2. When something bubbles, hisses, or lets out gas (like with soda).

Penelope has so much effervescence—her bubbly personality always brightens up the room.

flamboyant

(*flam-BOI-uhnt*), adjective
Bold, brilliant, elegant, and showy.

The peacock flaunted his flamboyant fleathers— whoops, I mean feathers.
Synonym: flashy

gadzooks

(*gad*-**ZOOKS**), interjection

Something you say when you're mad, upset, or surprised.

My parents promised me I could get any pet I wanted, but when I asked for a dog, they said I'd have to get a fish. Gadzooks!

Synonyms: egads, fiddlesticks

gimmick

(**GIM**-*ik*), noun

A plan, scheme, or gadget to make something irresistible.

The new minor league baseball team is giving away bobbleheads as a gimmick to sell tickets.

highfalutin

(*hie-fuh*-**LOOT**-*n*), adjective

Attempting to impress others with overdone and overly fancy words or ideas.

Alfred has a highfalutin friend who fakes a foreign accent and says he has been invited to tea with the Queen of England.

Synonyms: bombastic, grandiloquent, pompous

The Roots

You might think *gimmick* is a play on "gimme" because it makes you want something so badly. Its first known use goes back to 1911, but the word's true origin is unknown. One theory is that gimmick comes from "gimac," which is an *anagram* of the word "magic." This theory suggests the word was originally used to mean "a piece of magicians' equipment." Plus, con artists would use gimmicks, or tricks and schemes, to make people buy their products—or maybe because it's magical how a good *gimmick* makes you want something so badly!

hocus-pocus

(*HOH-kuhs-POH-kuhs*), noun or interjection

1. A nonsense phrase used by someone performing a magic trick.
2. An illusion or magic trick.
3. An activity to disguise trickery.

To perform this illusion, trust us, you must focus when you say "hocus-pocus!"

Synonym: abracadabra

hoity-toity

(*HOI-tee-TOI-tee*), adjective

Snobby. Acting overly important.

Alfred wants Penelope to dress all hoity-toity for the school dance, but she wants to wear her ripped jeans.

hooey

(*HOO-ee*), noun or interjection

Silly. Nonsense. Baloney.

That hooligan told you a bunch of hooey, so you shouldn't believe him!

Synonyms: balderdash, bunkum, fiddle-faddle, fiddledeedee, hogwash, hokum, horsefeathers, poppycock, tommyrot

horsefeathers

(*HORS-feh-therz*), interjection

Complete and utter nonsense.

Horsefeathers! Horses don't have feathers!

Synonyms: balderdash, bunkum, fiddle-faddle, fiddledeedee, hogwash, hokum, hooey, poppycock, tommyrot

humdinger

(*HUHM-ding-er*), noun
Something really cool
or excellent.
*Penelope had a humdinger
of a Sweet Sixteen! She
flew all her friends to Disney
World for the weekend!*

huzzah

(*huh-ZAH*), interjection or noun
A hurrah, praise, or
congratulation.
*It's the hundredth day
of school! Huzzah!*

The Roots

In mid-1800s slang, *hummer* described something so fast, it hummed as it passed by. (Think of a train.) *Ding* meant something that could "dent" something else, usually because of its size and strength. Expand that meaning a little, and "dinger" could mean anything that was bigger, stronger, and therefore better than other things. Put *hummer* and *dinger* together and you get *humdinger*, something fast, big, strong, and awesome!

HUZZAH!

I-N-D-O-M-I-T-A-B-L-E

indomitable

(*in-DOM-i-tuh-buhl*), adjective
Unstoppable or unconquerable.
*Penelope was an indomitable
force and won first place
in the Spelling Bee.*
Synonyms: invincible, juggernaut

ishkabibble

(*ISH-kuh-bib-uhl*), interjection
Something you say when you
think something isn't worth
worrying about. Sort of like
saying, "Fuggedaboutit!"
*It doesn't matter if you can't
find a fork—ishkabibble!
We're having pizza!*

Pop Culture

In the mid-1900s, comedian Merwyn Bogue created a funny character named Ish Kabibble. Bogue took the name from a song he used to sing on the radio, "Isch Ga-Bibble," but he spelled the name differently so it was easier to read and pronounce. In the song, the refrain "I should worry" is repeated umpteen times but used in a humorous way so it really means the opposite: "I shouldn't worry!" *Ishkabibble* was thought to come from Yiddish, but the closest Yiddish saying is *nisht gefidlt*, which doesn't seem that close. (Maybe if you say it fast or trip on your tongue, it sounds similar.) But *nisht gefidlt* means "it doesn't matter to me," and maybe that is just similar enough to "I shouldn't worry!" to make sense.

juggernaut

(*JUHG-er-nawt*), noun
Something unstoppable that will crush or defeat whatever gets in its way.
The lacrosse team is a juggernaut—they've gone undefeated all season long!
Synonyms: indomitable, invincible

The Roots

The story behind this word goes something like this: A monk visiting India reported seeing a huge wagon carrying a statue of the Hindu god Vishnu, who was called *Jagannath* in Sanskrit (*jagan* means "world," and *nath* means "protector"). As people lined the streets to pay respects to the religious symbol, the monk saw people crushed beneath the wagon's wheels—either in sacrifice to Vishnu or by accident. *Jagannath* morphed into *juggernaut*, and the meaning to a crushing, unstoppable force.

kaleidoscope

(*kuh-**LAHY**-duh-skohp*),
noun or verb

1. A cool gadget with a long tube you look through, with colorful doodads and mirrors that make beautiful patterns when turned.
2. Continually changing, especially in colorful patterns.

When the sun sets, the sky turns into a kaleidoscope of beautiful colors.

kerplunk

(*ker-**PLUHNGK***), noun or adverb
A dull, muffled noise something makes such as when it is dropped in water.
Penelope jumped off the high dive with a kerplunk into the pool.

The Roots

Kaleidoscopes can be toys or gorgeous pieces of art, but they were not invented by a toy maker or an artist! A Scottish scientist named Sir David Brewster was studying the properties of light and noticed that interesting patterns would form when he looked at objects as they reflected against two mirrors. He used the Greek words for "beautiful" (*kalos*), "shape" (*eodos*), and "watch" (*scopeo*) and called his new discovery a kaleidoscope—a beautiful shape to watch.

kowtow

(*KOW-TOW*), verb

To behave in a way that is overly flattering to someone you see as a leader. You're kissing up to get in with the big man.

You'd better kowtow to the captain of the kickball team—do anything he asks or he'll kick you off the team!

Synonyms: toady, bootlick, suck up

The Roots

Kowtow comes from the Chinese *ketou,* which literally means "knock the head." When the ancient Chinese bowed in front of a superior, they kneeled and bent forward until their head touched the floor. This low bow was a sign of respect. Now, to *kowtow,* you don't actually have to bonk your head on the ground, you just have to follow the leader.

nomophobia

(*noh-moh-**FOH**-bee-uh*), noun
The fear of being without your mobile phone.
I know what it's like to lose a phone—that's why I have nomophobia now.

outlandish

(*out-**LAN**-dish*), adjective
1. Odd, strange, and ridiculous.
2. Appearing out of place and from a foreign area.

My sister always wears outlandish hats to get people's attention.

Pop Culture

Nomophobia is one of the new words that the *Merriam-Webster Dictionary* added in April 2016. According to the lexicographers, the first use of the word was in 2008, just four years after the Apple iPhone was introduced. People had become so dependent on their smartphones so quickly, the word was created to describe the fear of being without one. (Talk about major FOMO—fear of missing out.) In order to be added to the dictionary, *nomophobia* had to be used repeatedly in common conversation and in print. It took about eight years for *nomophobia* to reach the level of popularity needed to appear in *Merriam-Webster's Dictionary*.

panache

(*puh-**NASH***), noun

A grand style and fancy flair.

Penelope flipped the pancakes with panache, twirling the spatula.

phantasmagorical

(*phan-taz-muh-**GAWR**-i-kuhl*), adjective

1. Fantastic, like something created by a dream or the imagination.
2. Changing appearance, either by magic or optical illusion.

Wow, the creature in that movie disappeared and reappeared with phantasmagorical special effects, swirling clouds, and colors that melted into one another.

pulchritudinous

(*puhl-kri-**TOOD**-n-uhs*), adjective

Most beautiful.

The trees after the ice storm glistened in white—it was a pulchritudinous sight!

Synonyms: gorgeous, stunning

The Roots

How can a word that sounds so ugly mean something so lovely? *Pulchritudinous* comes from the Latin root *pulcher*, which means "beautiful." But *pulcher* is such a clunker to say, it's no wonder that many beautiful words didn't follow. There's no *pulchy* or *pulchiful*...and maybe that's for the best!

pizzazz

(*pih-ZAZ*), noun

An energetic, lively quality that makes something attractive and glamorous.

The young actress has so much pizzazz, she wowed the audience from her first note to her last!

Synonyms: razzle-dazzle, razzmatazz

quiddity

(*KWID-i-tee*), noun

1. The essence of something, what makes something what it is.
2. An odd feature.
3. A silly point made in an argument that misses the *real* point.

Anne's red hair made her stand out and captured her fiery personality perfectly—it was the true quiddity of who she was.

razzmatazz

(*RAZ-muh-TAZ*), noun

Any showy thing or action that will attract attention.

When Penelope dances and sings, she performs with razzmatazz.

Synonyms: pizzazz, razzle-dazzle

Pop Culture

The *Oxford English Dictionary* says *pizzazz* was coined by Diana Vreeland, editor of fashion magazine *Harper's Bazaar* in the late 1930s. According to her, if a piece of clothing had excitement and energy to it, it oozed with *pizzazz*. However, other sources claim the word had been around since about 1910. *Pizzazz* has a similar meaning as *razzle-dazzle* and *razzmatazz*, and it also seems connected to jazz—which may be because that style of music was full of energy and popular at the time.

razzle-dazzle

(*RAZ-uhl-DAZ-uhl*), noun

Flash, glitz, bling, or excitement.

The cast's performance in the play was full of razzle-dazzle so the crowd gave them a standing ovation!

Synonyms: pizzazz, razzmatazz

resplendent

(*reh-SPLEN-duhnt*), adjective

Shining brightly and beautifully.

Alfred washed and waxed his bike until it was resplendent.

ripsnorter

(*RIP-snor-ter*), noun

1. Something strong and intense.
2. Something terribly exciting.

That upside-down and backward rollercoaster is a ripsnorter of a ride!

scintillating

(*SIN-tl-ey-ting*), adjective

1. Sparkling and exciting.
2. Witty and clever.

The circus performers thrilled us with scintillating skills on the trapeze.

spellbind

(**SPEL**-bahynd), verb

To fascinate someone so much that they feel like they're in a trance.

The magician wowed the crowd with spellbinding illusions.

Synonym: bewitch

spiffy

(**SPIF**-ee), adjective

Clean, neat, and well-dressed to impress.

Alfred can get spiffy in a jiffy. (Especially if he's on the way to see Penelope.)

Synonyms: dapper, dashing

splendiferous

(splen-**DIF**-er-uhs), adjective

Even better than splendid. Awesome.

Alfred's lemonade stand was splendiferous because he made lemonade from scratch, not with a powdered mix!

superfluous

(soo-**PUR**-floo-uhs), adjective

Something extra that's completely unnecessary (just like the word *completely* in this definition). Generally added on to draw more attention or seem more important.

Superman's cape is superfluous—he doesn't need it to fly; it just looks cool flapping in the wind.

DUMBFOUND BLINDSIDE

MUDDLE FLABBERGASTED

FLUMMOX BUMFUZZLE

BOGGLE GOBSMACKED

PERPLEXED KAPUT

SPIT TAKE INCREDULOUS

NONPLUSSED BEFUDDLE

SHOCK VALUE

Words to describe the surprising, confusing, and mindboggling

You've watched that magic trick be performed a million times, and you still can't figure out how it's done—it's left you *flummoxed*. You've been working on homework for hours and still don't get it—you're *befuddled*. You thought your friends had your back, but they don't—talk about being *blindsided*. You walk into the room when—surprise!—all your friends and family are there and ready to party! They've left you *gobsmacked* in the best possible way! There are a lot of things that might leave us confused, surprised, and amazed, but you no longer need to wonder at what word to use to describe your reactions!

befuddle

(*bih-FUHD-l*), verb

To confuse someone so badly they cannot think.

These complicated directions on the map befuddle me. (Oh, wait! I was holding it upside down!)

Synonyms: boggle, bumfuzzle, discombobulate, dumbfound, flummox, stupefy

blindside

(*BLAHYND-sahyd*), verb

To attack by surprise—you never see it coming.

The kids were walking home from school when they felt something hit their backs and got blindsided by a snowball fight.

Pop Culture

Blindside is a term used in football. When a defensive player tackles a quarterback from the side opposite his throwing arm, he can't see the attack coming, so he's been *blindsided!*

boggle

(*BOG-uhl*), verb

1. To be so amazed, you become overwhelmed and confused.
2. To bungle or mess something up.

When I think about the fact that there are one billion TRILLION stars in the universe, it boggles my mind!

Synonyms: befuddle, bumfuzzle, discombobulate, dumbfound, flummox, stupefy

Pop Culture

Boggle is a word game with sixteen letter cubes in a four-by-four grid. The object is to make words out of connecting letters—which have been all jumbled up and scrambled, so it's easy to become boggled! The more unique words you find, the more points you get.

bumfuzzle

(*BUHM-fuhz-uhl*), verb
Extremely confused.
Alfred gets bumfuzzled over the crossword puzzle
and usually gives up after just one clue!
Synonyms: befuddle, boggle, discombobulate,
dumbfound, flummox, stupefy

discombobulate

(*dis-kuhm-BOB-yuh-leyt*), verb
To confuse or frustrate someone.
Putting on a blindfold and spinning around before
hitting a piñata is meant to discombobulate you.
Synonyms: befuddle, boggle, bumfuzzle,
dumbfound, flummox, stupefy

dumbfound

(*duhm-FOUND*), verb
To amaze or shock into silence.
We were dumbfounded when the teacher told
us the Earth was 4½ billion years old.
Synonyms: befuddle, boggle, bumfuzzle, discombobulate, flummox, stupefy

flabbergasted

(*FLAB-er-gas-ted*), adjective
So shocked and surprised that all you can do is
stand there with your mouth hanging open.
Alfred was flabbergasted when he won front-row seats
to the concert that had been sold out for months!
Synonyms: gobsmacked, thunderstruck

flummox

(*FLUHM-uhks*), verb

To confuse someone terribly.

The difficult directions flummoxed my dad, so we showed up to the party two hours late.

gobsmacked

(*GOB-smakt*), adjective

Absolutely surprised and amazed.

I'm gobsmacked that I learned how to ice skate without holding onto the wall in just one lesson!

Synonym: flabbergasted

incredulous

(*in-KREJ-uh-luhs*), adjective

Showing doubt and disbelief.

Alfred spent three weeks studying and was incredibly incredulous over his poor report card.

Synonym: skeptical

kaput

(*kah-PUHT*), adjective

Finished, ruined, broken, done—game over.

Some kids want school to be kaput at noon, but that's before my favorite subject—lunch!

The Roots

Gob is British slang for "mouth," so *gobsmacked* means to be so surprised, you smack your mouth with your hand! OH!

muddle

(*MUHD-uhl*), verb

1. To mix up or confuse.
2. To make a mess of something.
3. To literally make something muddy.

Alfred muddled his lines, which muddled the play, so no one enjoyed it.

Synonyms: mess up, disorder

perplexed

(*per-PLEKST*), adjective

Pretty much the most baffled you can be.

I was sick and missed the new math lessons, so when I tried to make up the work, I got perplexed and stayed after school for help.

Synonyms: confused, nonplussed

nonplussed

(*non*-**PLUHST**), noun, verb, or adjective

1. *(noun)* A state of surprise and confusion.
2. *(verb)* To surprise or baffle someone.
3. *(adj.)* So completely surprised and confused that you don't know how to react.

Our trip to Boston had been planned for months, so when my mom said we were going to New York City instead, I was nonplussed.

Synonyms: baffled, perplexed

spit take

(**SPIT** *teyk*), noun

When you are surprised while sipping a drink and spit it out all over the place. Used by slapstick comics for a guaranteed laugh!

Penelope did a spit take at the lunch table and got chocolate milk all over Alfred!

stupefaction

(*stoo-puh*-**FAK**-*shuhn*), noun

A state of being so overwhelmed and amazed that you are stunned into a state of stupidity.

When I saw the gorilla doing sign language, I was numb with stupefaction! I had no idea we could communicate so clearly with animals!

thunderstruck

(**THUHN**-*der-struhk*), adjective

Amazed and astounded into silence.

Penelope was thunderstruck to learn that she had won the lead role in the school play even though she had never acted before!

Synonyms: befuddled, boggled, dumbfounded, flabbergasted, flummoxed, gobsmacked, stupefied

MAELSTROM

MAYHEM

RUCKUS

BABOONERY

HUBBUB

BALLYHOO

AMOK

BOISTEROUS

BROUHAHA

BONZO

FIASCO

BREAKNECK

RICOCHET

RUMPUS

WHAT A ZOO!

Words for all things rowdy, loud, and chaotic

A free-for-all dodgeball game is bound to be *mayhem*. Finding out school has been canceled might get you so excited, you go *berserk*! And a sleepover with all your friends is sure to be enough of a *hubbub* that your parents might need to ask you to quiet down. But if you can't occasionally get a little *rambunctious*, then what's the point of being a kid?

amok

(*uh-MUK*), adverb

Wild and out of control.

The students run amok when a substitute teacher takes over—they don't follow any of the instructions and the whole class falls into chaos.

baboonery

(*ba-BOO-nuh-ree*), noun

Silly behavior and actions; poking fun at something.

The teacher scolded the class at the zoo for acting like monkeys and making more baboonery than the baboons!

Synonym: tomfoolery

ballyhoo

(*BAL-ee-hoo*), noun

1. A loud uproar.
2. Advertising or promotion for a product or cause that goes to extreme, ridiculous lengths to convince people to buy it.

The crowd went wild and made a ballyhoo when the referee made a bad call and the home team lost the championship by one point.

bedlam

(*BED-luhm*), noun

Loud chaos and confusion.

When hockey players begin fighting on the ice, the whole arena breaks into bedlam.

Synonyms: chaos, mayhem

berserk

(*ber-ZURK*), adjective
Wild, crazy, and out of control.

Penelope went totally berserk when Alfred told her he had gotten her front-row tickets and a backstage pass to meet her favorite singer.

The Roots

Historians think the Old Norse words *ber serk* literally mean "bear shirt." Can you imagine if a bear had to wear a shirt, struggling to fasten all those tiny buttons? No wonder the beast went berserk!

But really, *berserkars* were a tribe of violent Vikings who wore bearskin clothing. So when Sir Walter Scott used the word *berserker* in his novel *The Pirate* in 1822, he used it to mean "violently angry." The shortened version *berserk*—to be wild and frenzied—became popularly used by midcentury and is still used today. (I suppose you can say folks went berserk for *berserk*.)

boisterous

(*BOI-ster-uhs*), adjective
Noisy and rowdy.
The boisterous hockey team banged their sticks as they stepped onto the ice for the last game of the season.

bonkers

(*BONG-kerz*), adjective
Out-of-control wild, enthusiastic, or annoyed.
You cannot eat chocolate anywhere near my sister, because she goes bonkers and won't leave you alone until you give her a bite!

bonzo

(*BAHN-zoh*), adjective
Even more wild or out of control.
The day before Christmas, the mall is a bonzo place to be—there are huge crowds rushing around.

breakneck

(*BREYK-nek*), adjective
Very dangerous, like traveling at a superfast speed. A wild ride.
Mom says I do breakneck tricks on my skateboard, and she's worried that one day I will break my neck. (Wait until she sees me on a snowboard!)

brouhaha

(*BROO-hah-hah*), noun

A noisy, chaotic commotion, especially about a specific thing or event.

There was a brouhaha when the baseball team's bus broke down and they didn't know how they would make it to the stadium on time.

Synonyms: hubbub, hurly-burly

careen

(*kuh-REEN*), verb

To tip over on one side and go out of control.

The go-cart was going so fast it careened and threw out the driver when it went around the corner.

The Roots

Brouhaha: Is it some sort of *onomatopoeia* or does it perhaps have its origins in Hebrew? Linguists haven't reached an agreement on this! Some think it is just an imitation of a noisy situation. But others think *brouhaha* is a distortion of the Hebrew phrase *baruch haba*—which means "blessed is the person who comes"—used as a welcome or greeting. The Jewish people are known for doing things in community, so if a lot of people arrived somewhere at once, it's likely it'll get noisy and confusing. Just like a *brouhaha*!

fiasco

(*fee-AS-koh*), noun

A huge failure.

The festival was an absolute fiasco because none of the scheduled artists or performers showed up!

harum-scarum

(*HAIR-uhm-SKAIR-uhm*),

adjective, adverb, or noun

1. *(adj./adv.)* Wild, out of control, and irresponsible.
2. *(noun)* A person or action that is unpredictable or reckless.

Preschoolers on a playground run around harum-scarum with dirty hands, snotty noses, and not a care in the world.

Synonyms: haphazard, headlong, helter-skelter, higgledy-piggledy, hurly-burly

Level Up!

The word *fiasco* in Italian means "bottle," which is a far cry from its meaning in English. There have been many explanations about how this happened, but a favorite is about two hundred years old and features glassblowers in Venice. They were responsible for making expensive vases and glass sculptures, but blowing glass isn't easy, and sometimes a piece would shatter or get damaged. Any damaged glass would be saved and used to make cheap bottles for everyday use. In other words, every *fiasco* came out of a failed piece of art.

hubbub

(**HUHB**-*uhb*), noun

Loud noise and commotion caused by a group of people.

There was a hubbub at the park on the first warm and sunny Saturday of spring—you had to wait on a long line for the paddle boats, miniature golf, and even the seesaw!

hurly-burly

(**HUR**-*lee*-**BUR**-*lee*), noun or adjective

Disorder, noise, confusion, or chaos.

My hair is such a mess when I wake up—it's like a curly hurly-burly.

Synonyms: haphazard, harum-scarum, helter-skelter, higgledy-piggledy

kerfuffle

(*ker*-**FUHF**-*uhl*), noun

A noisy shuffle or disruption caused by conflict.

The boys got into a kerfuffle at their sleepover—they destroyed their pillows and there were feathers everywhere! What a kerFLUFFle.

maelstrom

(*MEYL-struhm*), noun

1. A wild, whipping whirlpool.
2. A chaotic situation.

When you pull the plug on the bathtub, the water spinning down the drain is not powerful enough to be a maelstrom!

The Roots

Up in Norway, there's a series of strong whirlpools known as *maelstroms*, a name composed of two Dutch words: *malen* (to grind something up) and *stroom* (stream). Real maelstroms aren't that big and violent, but in 1841, Edgar Allen Poe wrote a scary story titled "A Descent into the Maelstrom" about a ship pulled into a dangerously wild whirlpool. Nevermore was *maelstrom* to be known as just a Nordic word.

mayhem

(*MEY-hem*), noun

Chaos, confusion, and disorder.

On Free Doughnut Day, the bakery is nonstop mayhem with people streaming in, pushing each other, and just grabbing whatever they want!

Synonym: bedlam

rambunctious

(*ram-BUHNGK-shuhs*), adjective

Loud, wild, and uncontrolled.

Our new puppy was so much more rambunctious than we were prepared for—we had our hands full keeping him from destroying everything in the house.

ricochet

(*RIK*-uh-shay), noun or verb
The act of bouncing off one surface, then another, then another, then another, then another... (Better watch out!)
The ball ricochets off the walls when we play catch in my bedroom.

ruckus

(*RUHK*-uhs), noun
Loud disorder.
The rugby team will raise a ruckus over that referee's wrong call.

rumpus

(*RUHM*-puhs), noun
A loud uproar.
"And now," cried Max, "let the wild rumpus start!" (That's from Where the Wild Things Are *by Maurice Sendak.)*

tumultuous

(*too-MUHL*-chyoo-uhs), adjective
Full of general, loud disorder.
We took the train into the city, and when we arrived, the station was tumultuous and confusing.

Pop Culture

Ping, ping, PING! That's the call of Ricochet Rabbit, a cartoon character from the 1960s. Sheriff of the Wild West town Hoop 'n' Holler, this speedy rabbit would bounce around solving crimes, followed (slowly) by his deputy, Droop-a-Long Coyote.

RECIPE FOR DISASTER

Words for when something is sloppy, clumsy, or a total hot mess

Let's be real for a moment: We are *all* sometimes a bit of a mess. We forget about that homework assignment until the day it's due, so our work is *pell-mell*—messy and clearly not our best. We didn't clean our room, and with clothes piled high and stuff scattered everywhere, it's what you can now call *frowsy*. And it's not just people who aren't always well put together. That house on the corner that's falling apart and most likely haunted? Call it *doddering* or *ramshackle*. And most homes have a junk drawer or closet to catch all the *mishmash* and *gallimaufry* no one knows what to do with. It's normal for things to be a bit crooked, disordered, and out of sorts at times, but your words don't have to be!

blooper

(*BLOO-per*), noun
An embarrassing mistake, usually one caught on film.
The actor flubbed his line so badly, he made a dozen bloopers before he could deliver the line with a straight face.

blunderbuss

(*BLUHN-der-buhs*), noun
Someone who makes clumsy mistakes.
The blunderbuss tripped over his feet, spilled his soda, then slipped and fell right in the puddle.

bungle

(*BUHNG-guhl*), verb
To make a ~~mishap error~~ mistake or to mess something up. (OOPS!)
The burglar bungled the bank robbery by calling an Uber for his getaway.
Synonym: botch

calamity

(*kuh-LAM-i-tee*), noun
A terrible disaster, a miserable event, or a serious misfortune.
A hurricane is a calamity for cities along the coast that get battered by high winds and flooding.
Synonyms: catastrophe, quagmire

The Roots

The word *blunderbuss* comes from a seventeenth-century musket that was terribly inaccurate. This forefather of the modern shotgun had a short barrel that was flared at the end, like a small trumpet. This meant the lead balls used as ammunition didn't always leave the musket in the long, straight line needed to make the gun's aim exact and precise. When the lead balls were unavailable, people loaded it with rocks and other irregular objects that would damage the barrel. The blunderbuss wasn't good for long-range shooting and didn't last long either.

catawampus (or cattywampus)

(*kat-uh-WOM-puhs*), adjective or adverb

1. Crooked, uneven, or off-center.
2. Moved or placed diagonally.

When Alfred learned how to ride a bike, his dad held on so he didn't ride catawampus and fall over.

Synonyms: askew, cock-a-hoop, cockeyed

cockeyed

(*KOK-ahyd*), adjective

1. Crooked, lopsided, tilted, twisted, or otherwise out of order.
2. Silly and foolish.
3. Having crossed eyes.

I draw lines all cockeyed unless I use a ruler to guide the pencil.

Synonyms: askew, catawampus, cock-a-hoop

dilapidated

(*dih-LAP-i-dey-tid*), adjective

Falling apart from being neglected or abandoned.

The neighborhood kids thought the dilapidated house with the broken windows was haunted.

Synonym: ramshackle

dilemma

(*dih-LEM-uh*), noun

A difficult choice, usually between two things, with neither one a perfect solution. Would a choice between three impossible things would be a trilemma?

Penelope received two invitations for the same day and couldn't decide which party to attend—what a dilemma!

doddering

(*DOD-er-ing*), adjective

Shaky and unsteady.

Uh-oh, that doddering waitress is carrying too many plates, and this won't end well, especially for my cheeseburger!

faux pas

(*foh PAH*), noun

A mistake or slipup, especially in a social situation.

If the Queen invites you to tea, don't make a faux pas like forgetting to bow and curtsy to her!

flyaway

(*FLY-uh-wey*), adjective

1. Loose, flowing, and free; windblown.
2. (to describe hair) Very thin, light, and untidy.
3. (to describe people) Flighty, unreliable, easily excitable.
4. Ready for flight.

Because she was always running around and playing outside, Jo had a flyaway look to her clothes and rarely looked neat and put-together.

foozle

(*FOO-zuhl*), verb

To bungle or to play a sport clumsily.

Alfred foozled the football and fumbled, so his teammates said he should stick to basketball.

frowsy

(*FROU-zee*), adjective

Dirty and smelly because it clearly has not been well taken care of.

Alfred's room is frowsy because he leaves dirty clothes and dirty dishes all over the place.

Synonyms: sloppy, untidy, unkempt

gallimaufry

(*gal-uh-MAW-free*), noun

A jumble of things.

When I grow up, I want to own a gallery to exhibit my collected gallimaufry of things—baseball cards, beach shells, homemade slime, and stuffed animals.

Synonym: hodgepodge, mishmash, potpourri

glitch

(*glich*), noun

An error or malfunction.

This video game keeps restarting at the level I already beat, and it's giving me a bunch of other glitches too, like erasing my score. I give up!

haphazard

(*hap-HAZ-erd*), adjective, adverb, or noun

Random, disorganized, or irregular.

The students shelved the books in haphazard order, instead of in alphabetical order. (How will they ever find them again?)

Synonyms: harum-scarum, helter-skelter, higgledy-piggledy, hurly-burly

The Roots

It's possible that *glitch* came from the Yiddish word *glitschen*, which means "slip" or "slip up." While the word still means any mistake or error in English, it's taken on a very technical meaning too. The first recorded usage in English was around the 1940s—radio broadcasters would say it whenever someone made an error. From radio it jumped to TV and telecommunications—industries that rely on the development of new technology. And new technology tends to have some problems until all the *glitches* get worked out.

Technology made space travel possible, and when astronaut John Glenn used "glitch" in the 1960s to describe problems with the mission to the moon, it's easy to see why *glitch* is now widespread (and still mostly used in relation to high-tech malfunctions).

headlong

(**HED**-lawng), adverb or adjective

1. Doing something without thinking it through.
2. Doing something immediately, quickly.
3. Moving in a direction with the head first.

Alfred skipped the instructions and dove headlong into building the spaceship model, but it collapsed and he had to start all over again.

Synonyms: impromptu, pell-mell, slapdash, willy-nilly

helter-skelter

(**HEL**-ter-**SKEL**-ter), adjective, adverb, or noun

Disorganized, disorderly, confused, or rushed. Phew!

The bus to pick up the team was an hour late, so they rushed on helter-skelter and forgot the pitcher in the parking lot.

Synonyms: haphazard, harum-scarum, higgledy-piggledy, hurly-burly

higgledy-piggledy

(**HIG**-uhl-dee-**PIG**-uhl-dee), adjective or adverb

Confused and disorderly.

The piglets scattered higgledy-piggledy when a goose got loose in their pen.

Synonyms: haphazard, harum-scarum, helter-skelter, hurly-burly

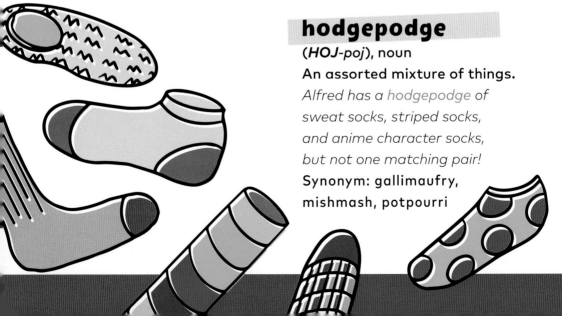

hodgepodge

(**HOJ**-poj), noun

An assorted mixture of things.

Alfred has a hodgepodge of sweat socks, striped socks, and anime character socks, but not one matching pair!

Synonym: gallimaufry, mishmash, potpourri

Level Up!

While Americans can understand British people and they can understand us (as long as our accents aren't too intense), our language is not exactly the same. The Brits have slang that we don't use—like *chuffed*, which means "to be extremely pleased." (You must be chuffed to know *chuffed*!) In England, they use the word *hotchpotch* instead of *hodgepodge*, where besides meaning "an assorted jumble of things," it's also a stew of mutton (sheep) and vegetables.

impromptu

(*im-PROMP-too*),
adjective or adverb
1. Done without preparation.
2. Done on the spur of the moment.

We built an impromptu igloo that caved in within minutes. (Maybe because we didn't plan it out first.)
Synonyms: headlong, impromptu, pell-mell, slapdash, willy-nilly

jargogle

(*jar-GO-guhl*), verb
To confuse and mix up; when things are jumbled and garbled.
Penelope's brain got jargogled while baking—she mixed up the salt and sugar and her cake tasted horrible!

madcap

(*MAD*-kap), adjective or noun
1. *(adj.)* Diving immediately into things without thinking about them first. Reckless and impulsive.
2. *(adj.)* A bit unusual or weird (but in a funny and enjoyable way).
3. *(noun)* Someone who is a daredevil, overconfident, and reckless.
4. *(noun)* Someone who is eccentric or very, very weird.

The princess had no interest in the princes who wanted to marry her, so she had the madcap idea to run away and become a dragon's princess instead! (And the whole kingdom thought she was a madcap.)

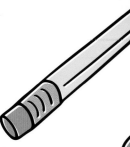

mishmash

(**MISH**-*mash*), noun

A mixed-up bunch of mismatched stuff.

The bottom of my backpack is a mishmash of granola crumbs, broken pencils, loose change, and crumpled paper.

Synonyms: gallimaufry, hodgepodge, potpourri

pell-mell

(**PEHL-MEHL**), adverb or adjective

Quick, hurried, confused, and disorderly. Launching into something without being ready.

We leapt over the fence pell-mell to get away from the galloping horses—but didn't notice the huge, muddy puddle on the other side.

Synonyms: headlong, impromptu, pell-mell, slapdash, willy-nilly

quagmire

(**KWAG**-*mahyuhr*), noun

A situation that's difficult to find a way out of.

I have to be at the soccer championship and the chess tournament at the same time—what a quagmire!

Synonym: dilemma

ragtag

(**RAG**-*tag*), adjective or noun

1. (*adj.*) Ragged, torn, and messy.
2. (*noun*) A mix of diverse, different things.

Penelope wears her dad's ragtag college sweats as pajamas, because even though they have holes, they're worn in, soft, and cozy.

ramshackle

(*RAM-shak-uhl*), adjective
Put together in a sloppy or careless way, so it
is likely to fall apart and collapse.
*Alfred built his ramshackle boxcar in one night, and when it was
time to race, it came apart before it could reach the finish line.*
Synonym: dilapidated

ransack

(*RAN-sak*), verb
To search for something thoroughly by tossing
things all over the place and making a mess.
*Alfred ransacked his room looking for his backpack,
throwing clothes, books, and papers everywhere.*

shambolic

(*sham-BOL-ik*), adjective
Disorganized, disordered, messy.
*My mom said my room was shambolic—but I
like keeping my clothes on the floor.*

slapdash

(*SLAP-dash*), adjective or adverb
Thrown together quickly and carelessly.
*Alfred got dressed in a slapdash rush this morning and
didn't notice he was wearing everything inside-out.*
Synonyms: headlong, impromptu, pell-mell, slapdash, willy-nilly

slipshod

(*SLIP-shod*), adjective
Messy, careless, and practically falling apart.
*Penelope did a slipshod job washing the dishes—
there was still food stuck on every plate!*

switcheroo

(*swich-uh-**ROO***), noun

A complete and sudden U-turn in direction, thought, or action.

Alfred got knocked around and did a switcheroo, running the wrong way down the field and scoring a touchdown for the other team!

topsy-turvy

(***TOP**-see-**TUR**-vee*), adjective or adverb

Upside down or all out of order and mixed up.

Our new puppy is having a tough time using the stairs—sometimes he misses a step, rolls backward, and lands topsy-turvy!

widdershins (or withershins)

(***WID**-er-shinz* or ***WITH**-er-shinz*), adverb

In a direction that is wrong, counterclockwise, or left-handed; opposite of what's expected.

Kayla really wished she had a GPS instead of this old-school compass—it made her go widdershins, and she kept going around in circles for hours!

The Roots

Widdershins comes from the German word *weddersinnes—wider* meant "against," and *sinnes* meant "to travel." There is also belief that the second half, *sinnes*, became confused with the Scottish word *sin* that means "sun," since before there were compasses or GPS satellites, people used the sun to point them in the right direction.

willy-nilly

(**WIL**-ee-**NIL**-ee), adverb or adjective
In a hurried, haphazard, unorganized way,
without much thought or planning.

*We can't just go to the beach all willy-nilly! We need sunscreen
and towels and chairs and shovels, and...we need to make a list!*

Synonyms: headlong, impromptu, pell-mell, slapdash, willy-nilly

wipeout

(**WHYP**-out), noun
A failure or a bad fall.

*The trick to avoiding a wipeout on the ice is to
not step onto the ice in the first place.*

wonky

(**WONG**-key), adjective
Unsteady, crooked, and shaky.

*Alfred looked pretty wonky as he tried to walk across
the ice—it was clear he'd never skated before!*

woozy

(**WOO**-zee), adjective
Dizzy and confused.

*When I wake up from an afternoon nap, I'm woozy for a minute, trying
to figure out if I slept through the entire night and it's the next day!*

SAY WHAT?

Words to describe the mysteries of the English language

If words spoke their own language, these terms would be part of their chats. They'd say that when someone is exaggerating, it's called *hyperbole*. Or that those little dots above some vowels can be called *umlauts*. You may not necessarily use these words in everyday conversation, but you can be the ultimate word expert (and impress all your English teachers) by learning the *lingo*, the *vernacular*, the language of language.

abecedarian

(ey-bee-see-**DAIR**-ee-uhn),
adjective and noun
1. *(adj.)* Anything related to the alphabet; arranged alphabetically.
2. *(noun)* Someone who's a beginner, or something that is at the beginning level or very basic.

The kindergarteners are abecedarians who are learning the abecedarian ABC song—but they keep getting the letters mixed up so it's no longer abecedarian!

Level Up!

Abecedarian is also a type of ancient poem where the first letter of each line or section follows alphabetical order—so in English, starting with A all the way down to Z. These types of poems were often used for spiritual and religious purposes like prayers and hymns as a device to help people remember them. Some poets today still use this style of writing!

ampersand

(**AM**-per-sand), noun
A symbol for the word "and" (&).
Alfred traced an ampersand in the sand between his name and Penelope's.

Level Up!

The word *ampersand* seems overly complex for a symbol that just means "and," but the truth is that *ampersand* is what we would call a *portmanteau*, or a word mash-up. While the symbol has been seen on stone tablets almost two thousand years old, it didn't have a name until fairly recently. In the early 1800s, a children's song to help them learn the alphabet included the line "and per se and," which became the word we know today. If you say "and per se and" ten times fast, it'll sound a lot like *ampersand*.

It's believed the look of the symbol is a morphed-together "e" and "t" for the Latin word *et*, which also meant "and."

anagram

(**AN**-uh-**GRAM**), noun

A word or phrase formed by rearranging
letters of another word or phrase.

*Anagrams are a hilarious way to create secret code
names—Penelope can be "Leon Peep."*

FUN ANAGRAMS

A decimal point = I'm a dot in place

The detectives = Detect thieves

Dormitory = Dirty room

Butterfly = Flutter-by

Garbage man = Bag manager

A gentleman = Elegant man

Listen = Silent

Snooze alarms = Alas! No more Zs

Can you come up with more anagrams? Your name is a good
place to begin...

aphthong

(**AF**-thawng), noun

A letter or group of letters in a word that
are silent and not pronounced.

*The letter "e" in motorbike is an aphthong, but the
motorbike itself is the loudest thing I ever heard!*

cliché

(*klee-SHEY*), noun or adjective

1. *(noun)* An expression or phrase that is overused and common.
2. *(adj.)* Lacking originality.

Telling the teacher the dog ate your homework is such a cliché!

Synonym: (adj.) hackneyed, trite; (noun) aphorism, chestnut

colloquialism

(*kuh-LOH-kwee-uh-liz-uhm*), noun

An expression or phrase that is common
only to a specific region or area.

If you're going to the beach in New Jersey, use the colloquialism "go down the shore" instead.

cryptonym

(*KRIP-tuh-nim*), noun

A code word or name.

To be allowed into the secret club, you have to know the cryptonym.

denouement

(*DEY-noo-MAHN*), noun

The part of a story between the climax and the end: the resolution.

Your teacher will be impressed if you can point out the denouement in the book.

diphthong

(*DIF-thawng*), noun

Two or more letters which, when read together, make a single sound.

The sounds "ou" in "sound" and "oy" in "toy" are diphthongs.

eggcorn

(*EG-korn*), noun

A word or phrase that sounds similar to another word or phrase but is wrong—it happens when the real word or phrase has been misheard.

Penelope's little sister is always using eggcorns—she calls caterpillars "callapitters" and recently got the chicken pox but kept saying she had the "chicken spots."

Synonyms: malapropism, mondegreen

Common Eggcorns

EGGCORN	CORRECT WORD OR PHRASE
A washed pot never boils	A watched pot never boils
Bob wire	Barbed wire
Cut to the cheese	Cut to the chase
Duck Tape (brand name)	Duct tape
Hearbuds	Earbuds
I knew it from the gecko	I knew it from the get-go
Jig-solve puzzle	Jigsaw puzzle
Nip it in the butt	Nip it in the bud
Platemat	Placemat
Sick sense	Sixth sense
Wheelbarrel	Wheelbarrow

endonym

(*EN-doh-nim*), noun

A name for a place used by locals and not by visitors of that place.

Some people use the endonym Chi-Town for the city in Illinois known as Chicago.

epistrophe

(*ih-PIS-truh-fee*), noun

The repetition of a word at the end of a sentence or clause.
Generally used to emphasize whatever point you're trying to make.

*"I can't wait for summer. I love summer. I live for
summer!" Alfred said, using epistrophe to make sure
we all got how much summer meant to him.*

exonym

(*EK-soh-nim*), noun

A name for a place used by foreigners and
not by the residents of that place.

*Americans use the exonym Naples for the city
in Italy known to locals as Napoli.*

grawlix

(*GRAH-licks*), noun

The symbols used to replace
curse words in writing,
especially common in comics.

*Alfred's grandpa has a potty
mouth, and Alfred had to use a
lot of grawlixes to quote grandpa
in his assignment for school.*

Level Up!

Grawlixes are a type of
"maledicta," or any kind
of bad language. *Male-
dicta* comes from putting
together Latin words for
"bad" (*mal*) and "saying"
(*dicta*). Kids aren't supposed to use bad language,
so grawlixes were used to
replace them in anything
adults thought young eyes
might see. Other types of
maledicta are *jarns*, *nittles*,
and *quimps*.

hackneyed

(*HAK-need*), adjective
Overused and unoriginal.

Listening to a lecture from my uncle is the worst—he uses so many hackneyed phrases, like we haven't heard it all before!
Synonym: cliché

hyperbole

(*hahy-PUR-buh-lee*), noun
A ridiculous exaggeration not to be taken literally.

"I'm so hungry I could eat a horse," Alfred said. Penelope didn't realize he was speaking in hyperbole and was afraid to let him get near her pony.

idiom

(*ID-ee-uhm*), noun
A common saying or phrase, often having a meaning different than what it sounds like.

Alfred is always confused when people use idioms and can't understand why people can't say exactly what they mean.

The Roots

Idioms are a way for people to play with language—we twist the meaning of words in a fun and creative way so that it means something new. Idioms are best understood by native speakers of the language, because they rely on your understanding context and cultural norms. Different languages have their own idioms, which wouldn't necessarily make sense if they were translated into other languages. The word-for-word translation doesn't capture the special meaning of the phrase! Even if people speak the same language, being from a different region might mean you have different idioms—they don't "speak the same language" even though they speak the same language! (What???)

Here are some common American idioms:

"We speak the same language."	"We understand each other."
"It's a piece of cake."	"It's easy."
"Best thing since sliced bread."	"That's a genius idea!"
"You can't judge a book by its cover."	"You can't judge something by its appearance."
"It leaves a bad taste in my mouth."	"I don't like it."
"Heads up!"	"Watch out!"
"She's under the weather."	"She's sick."
"You missed the boat!"	"You missed your chance!"
"He's on the fence."	"He can't make the decision."
"Kill two birds with one stone."	"Accomplish two different tasks at the same time."
"Heard it through the grapevine."	"Heard a rumor."
"Actions speak louder than words."	"What you do tells more than what you say."
"Every cloud has a silver lining."	"Something good will come out of every bad situation."

interrobang

(*in-TER-uh-bang*), noun

A punctuation mark that combines the question mark and exclamation point. Used to declare an unbelievable surprise.

The character in the story was surprised and confused at the same time, so the author used an interrobang at the end of her dialogue.

Pop Culture

Martin K. Speckter invented the interrobang in a 1962 article for *Type Talks* magazine. The mark combines the question mark and exclamation point into one convenient symbol. The term *interrobang* is a mash-up of two words—*interrogate*, which means "to question" and *bang*, which is slang for an exclamation mark. (*Type Talks* readers suggested names like "exclamaquest," but "interrobang" is the term that Speckter settled on.) Although some typewriter manufacturers added the interrobang to their machines, the new punctuation mark never became popular. People didn't use it regularly enough, so it eventually was taken off all typing keypads. You may not have an interrobang key on your computer keyboard, but if you need to, you can still express doubt and excitement in a single sentence. You just have to use two symbols—the question mark and exclamation point—instead of one. (I know what you're thinking: But which one goes first?)

izzard

(*IZ-erd*), noun

An old name for the letter Z.

When I draw a cartoon with a character sleeping, I use a lot of izzards in the speech bubble.

Level Up!

You may have heard the letter *z* referred to as "zed" by the British or Canadians (or every other English-speaking country besides America). That's because the name was taken from the Middle French *zede*, which came from the Greek *zeta*. It's believed we Americans changed the pronunciation to "zee" because many of our other letters are pronounced similarly ("bee, cee, dee"), and so it rhymes with the last line of the Alphabet Song: "Next time won't you sing with me." The word *izzard*, which is infinitely more fun to say than either *zed* or *zee*, morphed from the Old French saying *et zede*, which means "and zee."

jargon

(*JAHR-guhn*), noun

Language and terms that are used in a specific industry.

Scientists love speaking in jargon, even though all the non-scientists have no clue what they are talking about.

juxtaposition

(*juhk-stuh-puh-ZISH-uhn*), noun

The placement of two things close to each other, sometimes for the purpose of comparing and contrasting them.

If you put the twins in juxtaposition, you could tell they aren't identical—one has blue eyes and the other has green eyes.

lingo

(*LING-goh*), noun

The words and language of a specific group or activity. Like *jargon*, but *lingo* is a slang term.

Danny doesn't understand any of the sports lingo, so he's always a bit lost when his friends are talking about last night's game.

mondegreen

(*MON*-dih-green), noun

A phrase that has been misheard—and then repeated over and over the wrong way. *Mondegreen* usually means misheard song lyrics.

My mom tries to be cool and sing along with songs on the radio, but she gets all the words wrong and just sings mondegreens instead. It's soooo embarrassing!

Synonym: eggcorn

Common Mondegreens

SONG & ARTIST	MISHEARD LYRIC	ACTUAL LYRIC
"Chasing Pavements" by Adele	"Or should I keep chasing penguins"	"Or should I keep chasing pavements"
"We Will Rock You" by Queen	"Kicking your cat all over the place"	"Kicking your can all over the place"
"Good for You" by Selena Gomez	"I'm farting carrots"	"I'm 14 carat"
"Lucy in the Sky with Diamonds" by the Beatles	"Blue seal in the sky with diamonds"	"Lucy in the sky with diamonds"
"Tiny Dancer" by Elton John	"Hold me closer, Tony Danza"	"Hold me closer, tiny dancer"
"Blank Space" by Taylor Swift	"Gotta love these Starbucks lovers"	"Got a long list of ex-lovers"
"Cups (When I'm Gone)" by Anna Kendrick	"You're gonna miss me by my walk, you're gonna miss me by my taco"	"You're gonna miss me by my walk, you're gonna miss me by my talk, oh"

mnemonic

(*ni-MON-ik*), adjective or noun
Something to help you remember, typically phrases or rhymes that are fun and easy to recall.

Penelope uses the mnemonic device "My Very Educated Mother Just Served Us Noodles" to remember the order of the planets—Mercury, Venus, Earth, Mars, Jupiter, Saturn, Uranus, and Neptune.

nomenclature

(*NOH-muhn-kley-cher*), noun
Terms and phrases used in a specific field, like in science or government.

We learn nomenclature for the branches of government in social studies—executive branch, legislative branch, and judicial branch.

octothorpe

(*AWK-tah-thor-p*), noun
The # symbol. Also known as the pound sign.

People used to use the octothorpe to mean "number," but now with social media, it's used for hashtags.

Level Up!

The @ symbol is called "at" in English, but it has some fun names and meanings in other languages!

LANGUAGE	WORD FOR @
Afrikaans	aapstert (monkey tail)
Armenian	shnik (puppy)
Bosnian	ludo (crazy A)
Danish	snabel-a (Elephant's trunk A)
Finnish	kissanhäntä (cat's tail)
Greek	papaki (duckling)
Hungarian	kukac (worm)
Italian	chiocciola (snail)
Vietnamese	còng (bent A) or móc (hooked A)

onomatopoeia

(*on-uh-mah-tuh-**PEE**-uh*), noun

A word that sounds like a sound.

Comic books are known for onomatopoeia—like whoosh, bam, zoom, and bonk!—to highlight the action happening on the page.

oxymoron

(*ok-si-**MAWR**-on*), noun

Word or words within a phrase that contradict itself.

Zombies are oxymorons—how can something be living and dead?!

Fun Oxymorons

awfully **nice**, *baby* **grand**, *dark* **star**, *even* **odds**, *freezer* **burn**, *good* **grief**, *high* **ground**, *inside* **out**, *jumbo* **shrimp**, *long* **shorts**, *mud* **bath**, *never* **again**, *old* **news**, *pretty* **ugly**, *quiet* **storm**, *random* **order**, *seriously* **funny**, *top* **floor**, *upside* **down**, *virtual* **reality**, *whole* **piece**, *young* **adult**.

palindrome

(*PAL*-in-drohm), noun

A number, word, name, sentence, or anything that reads the same forward as it does backward.

Mom and Dad are palindromes. So is Sis but not Bro. (Poor Bro feels left out!)

The Roots

Wouldn't it make a lot of sense if *palindrome* were a palindrome itself? Like *kayak*? Or *racecar*? Unfortunately, *palindrome* backward is "emordnilap"—definitely not the same! But once you learn its Greek origin, you'll realize the word is perfect as it is. *Palin* means "again," and *dramein* means "to run." Put them together and you have "to run again." OK, Greek, you win again!

phantonym

(*FAN*-ton-im), noun

A word that sounds like it means one thing but really means something else. In other words, a confused word. (Was that less confusing?)

Penelope told Alfred that she thought he was invaluable to the team. But because the prefix in- can mean "not," it was a phantonym to him, so Alfred thought he wasn't needed!

Level Up!

Phantonym is a word...that isn't exactly a word yet. A *New York Times* reporter named Jack Rosenthal coined it in 2009, but its use has not been widespread enough to land it into major English dictionaries.

This kind of word is called a *neologism*—it's new and in the process of officially entering the language.

PHANTONYM	SOUNDS LIKE IT MEANS	ACTUALLY MEANS
Boilerplate	A plate (lid) for a boiling pot	Standard terms in a contract
Enormity	Extremely large	Extremely evil
Invaluable	Has no value	Has so much value you can't even give it a value!
Jargogle	Goggles made from jars	To confuse
Lackey	Without a key	An assistant or servant
Noisome	Noisy	Smelly
Penultimate	Topnotch	Next to last
Phantonym	Phantom that looks like another phantom	Word that sounds like it means something it doesn't
Portmanteau	Poor man's toe	Word made from a blend of other words
Sockeroo	What you yell when you find a lost sock	A huge success
Spoonerism	Stuff you eat with a spoon	Mixing up the first syllables of two or more words
Suffrage	Suffering	The right to vote
Superfluous	A super fluid	Unnecessary
Whippersnapper	Someone who snaps a whip	Young person who is not ready
Winsome	Winning often	Being nice and charming

portmanteau

(*pawrt-MAN-toh*), noun

1. A new word made from a blend of two already existing words.
2. A large suitcase.

I bet my family created the portmanteau "staycation,"
'cause we always stay right here every vacation!

The Roots

Did you know *portmanteau* is a portmanteau itself? Originally, the word was used to mean a type of luggage (from the French words *porter* (carry) and *manteau* (mantle/covering)—so basically a covering you can carry). The word took on its new meaning when Lewis Carroll used it in *Through the Looking Glass, and What Alice Found There*, the sequel to *Alice's Adventures in Wonderland*. As luggage, the portmanteau had two large pockets of equal size that allowed the user to pack two things into one bag. So when Alice asked Humpty Dumpty to explain the words in the nonsense poem "Jabberwocky" to her, he says some of the words are "like a portmanteau—there are two meanings packed up into one word." English speakers soon began calling words that had been blended together *portmanteaux*!

spoonerism

(*SPOO-nuh-riz-uhm*), noun
Mixing up the first letters and sounds of two or more words in a row.
Roald Dahl loved using spoonerisms like "catasterous disastrophe" in his stories.

tittle

(*TIH-tl*), noun
1. The dot on top of a lowercase i or j.
2. A very tiny part of something.

Alfred always forgot to add the dot to his i's, while Penelope also used hearts instead of a tittle.

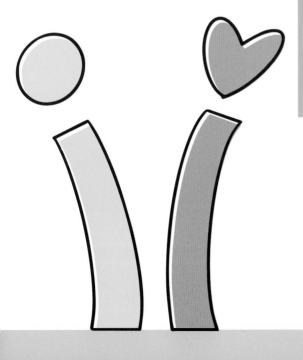

The Roots

Reverend William Archibald Spooner suffered frequent trips of the tongue during his lectures at Oxford University in the late 1800s. He would accidentally swap the beginning sounds of words. Not all his (hilarious) mistakes have been verified, but he is thought to have said things like "You have hissed all my mystery lectures" instead of "You have missed all my history lectures." These kinds of silly slipups were named after him and became well known as *spoonerisms* by the 1920s.

umlaut

(**OOM**-lout), noun

The two little dots above vowels in some languages, used to note a certain pronunciation.

English doesn't use any accents on letters, but words borrowed from other languages, like über from German, should keep their original umlaut above the u.

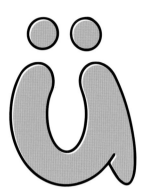

vernacular

(ver-**NAK**-yuh-ler), noun

The ordinary language and common speaking style of a group of people.

Adults don't understand teenage vernacular—and I don't understand the slang they use either!

wordplay

(**WURD**-pley), noun

A joke or funny statement based on being clever with words...or a play on words, like a pun.

Here's some wordplay for you: Whale hello there! Ewe are amazing!

RANDOM LANGUAGE FACTS

► *E* is the most commonly used letter in English.

► The most common English words are *I* and *you*.

► If you spelled out every number, you wouldn't use the letter "B" until you reached "one billion."

► Readers of fiction are exposed to a larger variety of vocabulary than nonfiction readers.

► The U.S. doesn't have an official language, though it's assumed to be English.

► The word *alphabet* comes from the first two letters of the Greek alphabet, *alpha* and *beta*.

► The word *bookkeeper* is the only non-hyphenated English word to have three double letters in a row (besides *bookkeeping*).

► A sentence that uses all twenty-six letters of the alphabet is called a *pangram*.

► "I am" is the shortest full sentence in English.

► There are 1.5 billion English speakers in the world.

SESQUIPEDALIAN

CRAMBO   VERBOMANIA

LOGOPHILE   WORDSMITH

ONOMATOMANIA

MUMPSIMUS   MANIFESTO

POETASTER   PSEUDONYM

LEXICOGRAPHER

WORD NERDS

Words for budding writers, passionate readers, and other lovers of language

Want to work on dictionaries when you're older? Then you dream of being a *lexicographer*. Hope to be a great poet but currently stink at it? Don't worry, with practice you'll outgrow being a *versemonger*. Clearly you have a love for words—you have *verbomania* or *onomatomania*—otherwise you probably wouldn't be reading this book! Whether your love stems from the delight of reading, the joy of writing, or the pleasure of correcting someone who uses words all wrong, become even more of a *wordsmith* with the words below.

anonymuncule

(*uh-NON-eh-muhn-kyool*), noun
A long-lost uncle. (Just kidding.)
An unimportant, unknown
writer. It's a blend of
anonymous and *homunculus*
(Latin for "tiny person").
*A long time ago, many women
writers were anonymuncules—no
one considered them important
enough to give them credit!*

biblioklept

(*BIB-lee-uh-klept*), noun
Someone who steals books.
*Ginny loves books so much, so
even though it's wrong to steal,
she can't help but be a biblioklept.*

boilerplate

(*BOI-ler-pleyt*), noun
Standard wording in a
letter, contract, or other
important document.
*Teachers always include a
space for your name and the
date on assignments—it's the
boilerplate for every worksheet.*

crambo

(*KRAM-boh*), noun
1. A game where players
   must rhyme with a line
   given by another team.
2. Rhyme that doesn't
   completely rhyme or sounds
   clunky and awkward.
*Don't play crambo on my
brother's team, because he thinks
spaghetti rhymes with fluffy.*

Level Up!

Crambo comes from the
Latin word *crambe*, which
means "cabbage." Cab-
bage? What does that
have to do with rhyming?!

It's believed that because
a lot of people don't like
cabbage, the word came
to mean anything distaste-
ful. And when you recite
terrible rhyme, it leaves a
bad taste in your mouth,
doesn't it? Blech!

floccinaucinihilipilification

(*flok-suh-naw-suh-nhy-hil-uh-pil-uh-fi-**KAY**-shuhn*), noun

The act or habit of deciding that something has little or no value.

Penelope really wanted to use the word floccinaucinihilipilification in their presentation, but Alfred thought it was floccinaucinihilipilification and not worth doing.

The Roots

Floccinaucinihilipilification is one of the longest words in the English language. In fact, it's the longest nontechnical one (which means it's not connected to any academic subjects or professional work). However, this word's length is pretty ridiculous, since its origin comes from putting together four Latin words that all mean exactly the same thing. *Flocci, nauci, nihili,* and *pili* all mean "at little value." Tag on the suffix *-fication* (which just lets you know this is a noun formed from a verb) and you get you get *flocci-nauci-nihili-pili-fication*. The word is rarely ever used in actual speech or writing.

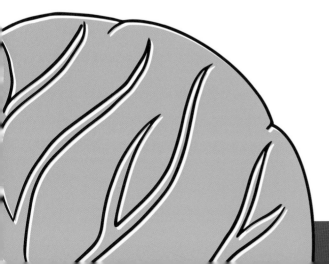

Breaking Down Long Words

Many of the looooongest words in English are medical and scientific terms, 'cause they generally smush together a bunch of Latin or Greek words. You can decode the meaning of these words thanks to prefixes and suffixes, like *anti-* or *non-* (which mean "not," "without," or "against"), or *-ness* (used to describe a condition). You can also figure out the meaning by breaking the word up into parts: Hippopotomonstrosesquipedaliophobia is a long word that means "fear of long words." You can tell it's a fear because it uses the word *phobia*. But someone was being silly when they added parts of *hippopotamus* and *monstrous* to the beginning of the word. Those aren't really prefixes; they just add letters and make the word a little more frightening. You may be asking about the *sesquipedalio* part of the word... so look it up! Sesquipedalian is right here in this book.

lexicographer
(lek-si-KOG-ruh-fer), noun
Someone who writes or edits a dictionary.
Penelope's dream job would be a lexicographer—she hopes to discover hundreds of more words to add to the dictionary!

logophile
(LAW-guh-fahyl), noun
Someone who loves words.
If you're reading this book, you might be a logophile.
(Come on, you ARE a logophile, aren't you?)

manifesto

(*man-uh-**FES**-toh*), noun

The ideas, goals, or beliefs of a person, country, or organization. Someone must believe the manifesto strongly, because to be a manifesto, it must be written out and shared publicly.

In order to make sure everyone knew what they stood for, the environmental club wrote out a manifesto.

mumpsimus

(***MUHMP**-suh-muhs*), noun

A believer of unreasonable things, such as someone who incorrectly uses a word or phrase over and over and refuses to be corrected.

Penelope's little sister is such a mumpsimus! We told her the phrase was "dog-eat-dog world," but she insists on saying "doggy-dog world" instead!

onomatomania

(*on-uh-mah-tuh-**MEY**-nee-uh*), noun

1. A craze for certain words.
2. A need to remember a certain word.

Penelope carries a dictionary everywhere she goes because she has onomatomania and is obsessed with knowing what words mean!

poetaster

(***POH**-uh-tass-ter*), noun

An awful poet.

Alfred is a poetaster—all his poems make absolutely no sense!

Synonyms: rhymester, versemonger

pseudonym

(**SOOD**-n-im), noun

A fake name an author uses to hide his or her identity.

Benjamin Franklin once published a series of humorous letters under a female pseudonym, Mrs. Silence Dogood—no one knew it was him until years later!

The Roots

Why are there so many "-onym" words? You may already know *homonym*, *antonym*, and *synonym* (be careful not to mispronounce it as "cinnamon")...but by now you probably have discovered *cryptonym*, *exonym*, *phantonym*, and *pseudonym*. The suffix -onym is taken from the Greek word for "name."

rhymester

(**RHYM**-ster), noun

Someone who writes terrible poetry.

Alfred hoped to woo Penelope with his poetry—but he is a rhymester, and Penelope thought all his poems were horrible.

Synonyms: poetaster, versemonger

sesquipedalian

(ses-kwih-pih-**DEY**-lee-uhn), adjective

1. Given to using very long words with a lot of syllables.
2. Having many syllables.

The sesquipedalian teacher knows so many long, multisyllabic words that sometimes it seems like she isn't even speaking English!

verbomania

(**VUR**-boh-**MEY**-nee-uh), noun

A state of being crazy for words and using a lot of them.

After reading this book, you may get a bad case of verbomania—you won't be able to stop learning more and more and more.

versemonger

(*VURS-muhng-ger*), noun

Someone who is terrible at writing poetry.

Penelope tried to show Alfred how to write better poetry, but it turned out she was a versemonger herself!

Synonyms: poetaster, rhymester

wordmonger

(*WURD-muhng-ger*), noun

Someone who throws words around willy-nilly, without knowing their true meaning.

Amy is always trying to use big words, but she's a wordmonger and it is clear she doesn't know what any of them actually mean.

wordsmith

(*WURD-smith*), noun

1. An expert word user, word writer, or word player.
2. Someone who writes for a living, like an author or journalist.

You've finished this section—now you can be a wordsmith and wow your friends with your expert use of words and language!

LILLIPUTIAN GALUMPH

JABBERWOCKY

MICAWBER POLLYANNA

PANDEMONIUM

QUIXOTIC LILY-LIVERED

MALAPROPISM

SCARAMOUCHE POOBAH

ONCE UPON A TIME...

Words that have remarkable origins in phenomenal stories and classic tales

Did you know that Dr. Seuss made up the word *nerd* when he wrote *If I Ran the Zoo* in 1950? Or that the poet and playwright William Shakespeare is responsible for over 1,500 words that are now part of the English language? We need words to help create stories, but stories also help create new words! Discover some weird and wonderful words below that have their roots in fabulous story-telling. And don't be scared—or *lily-livered*, as Shakespeare would say. Get inspired to create some new words yourself!

galumph

(*guh-LUHMF*), verb

To walk with heavy, clumsy footsteps. *Galumph* is thought to be a combination of *gallop + triumph* from its use in Lewis Carroll's poem "Jabberwocky."

After chopping off the knight's head and leaving him for dead, the giant went galumphing back into his cave.

jabberwocky

(*JAB-er-wok-ee*), noun

Nonsense, invented words, and language that sound close to real English.

Because it was a lot of jabberwocky, after reading the poem, Alice said, "It seems very pretty, but it's rather hard to understand."

Synonyms: babble, bafflegab, gibberish, gobbledygook

The Roots

"Jabberwocky" is a nonsense poem by Lewis Carroll, featured in his 1871 novel *Through the Looking Glass, and What Alice Found There* (the sequel to *Alice's Adventures in Wonderland*). The wondrous thing about the poem is that when you read it aloud, the sounds of the playful, made-up words make just enough sense to hint that it is about the slaying of a dangerous creature called the Jabberwock.

JABBERWOCKY by Lewis Carroll

'Twas brillig, and the slithy toves
    Did gyre and gimble in the wabe:
All mimsy were the borogoves,
    And the mome raths outgrabe.
"Beware the Jabberwock, my son!
    The jaws that bite, the claws that catch!
Beware the Jubjub bird, and shun
    The frumious Bandersnatch!"
He took his vorpal sword in hand;
    Long time the manxome foe he sought—
So rested he by the Tumtum tree
    And stood awhile in thought.
And, as in uffish thought he stood,
    The Jabberwock, with eyes of flame,
Came whiffling through the tulgey wood,
    And burbled as it came!
One, two! One, two! And through and through
    The vorpal blade went snicker-snack!
He left it dead, and with its head
    He went galumphing back.
"And hast thou slain the Jabberwock?
    Come to my arms, my beamish boy!
O frabjous day! Callooh! Callay!"
    He chortled in his joy.
'Twas brillig, and the slithy toves
    Did gyre and gimble in the wabe:
All mimsy were the borogoves,
    And the mome raths outgrabe.

Lilliputian

(*lil-i-PYOO-shuhn*),
adjective or noun
1. (*adj.*) Teeny-tiny.
2. (*adj.*) Not important.
3. (*noun*) A person who resides in Lilliput.
4. (*noun*) A teeny-tiny person.

Alfred is six foot two and too tall to be called a Lilliputian.

The Roots

In the novel *Gulliver's Travels* by Jonathan Swift, the main character, Gulliver, is in a shipwreck and washes up onshore in a fictional island nation known as Lilliput. Gulliver, whom the islanders fear is an evil giant, awakens tied up, tied down, and surrounded by the miniature people: Lilliputians! After the book's publication in 1726, the word soon grew to mean "tiny."

lily-livered

(*LIL-ee-LIV-erd*), adjective
Easily scared. Cowardly. Having no nerve!

The lily-livered boy ran away from the lily when he spotted a bumblebee.

Synonym: pusillanimous

The Roots

In the middle ages, the liver was believed to be in charge of our emotions, especially courage. Those with rosy red livers were healthy, strong, and brave. A lily is a white flower and was often used to describe someone who was pale, and therefore unhealthy. When someone was called lily-livered, it meant their liver was white and sick—and therefore, they were cowardly. Shakespeare coined the word in his play *Macbeth*, written in 1605.

malapropism

(*MAL*-uh-prop-iz-uhm), noun
A word that sounds close to
the right word—but is definitely
wrong—making a statement
seem preposterous and hilarious.

*Everyone laughed at Alfred's
malapropism when he
told Penelope that actions
speak louder than birds.*

Synonyms: eggcorn, mondegreen

The Roots

Mrs. Malaprop is a comedic character in the 1775 play *The Rivals* by Richard Brinsley Sheridan. She mistakenly utters words that are similar in sound to the correct ones, but they do not have similar meanings! Her statements tumble out as nonsense. (Her name is even a play on the word *malapropos*, which means "not appropriate.") Mrs. Malaprop exclaims, "He is the very pineapple of politeness!" Oops. She should have said "pinnacle" instead of the tropical fruit. Poor Mrs. Malaprop—she will forever be remembered in literary history as a ridiculous wordmonger, as the term *malapropism* is named after her.

Micawber

(*mih-**CAH**-bur*), noun
Someone who is poor
but believes good
fortune will happen.

John is such a Micawber—what little money he has he spends on lottery tickets, sure that one day he'll win millions!

The Roots

Mr. Wilkins Micawber is an ever-hopeful charac-ter in Charles Dickens's 1850 novel *David Copper-field*. He has problems with money, which land him in prison. But the poor man remains optimistic that his fortunes will improve. One of his favorite phrases is "something will turn up." *Micawber* is now used as a word that means some-one who expects better things, someone who is optimistic—maybe a little too optimistic despite their circumstances.

milquetoast

(*MILK*-tohst), noun

Someone extremely shy. They lack confidence and back down easily.

The milquetoast boy was afraid to tell Penelope she couldn't try his hoverboard, so he let her borrow it all week long.

The Roots

Harold T. Webster created the comic strip *The Timid Soul*, featuring a shy character loosely based on himself: Caspar Milquetoast. Mr. Milquetoast's comedic adventures, which began in the 1920s, painted him as a lily-livered nudnik. In one cartoon, his hat falls on a patch of grass a few feet away, next to a park sign: "KEEP OFF THE GRASS." Instead of grabbing his hat, Mr. Milquetoast decides to buy a new one! About a decade after the comic strip began, the word *milquetoast* began appearing in the English language to mean anyone who lacks confidence.

An easy way to remember this word: *Milquetoast* sounds like the bland, soggy dish known as "milk toast"—buttered toast in a dish of milk. A person who is milquetoast is mild and limp just like milk toast! (I bet Mr. Milquetoast would not send burnt milk toast back.)

pandemonium

(*pan-duh-**MOH**-nee-uhm*), noun
CHAOS!

*When a bunch of pandas
are let loose to play, you can
call it PANDAmonium.*

Level Up!

If you look closely at
the word *pandemonium*,
you'll see a nasty little
word hiding in the middle:
DEMON! Yikes! That's
because *pandemonium* is
a word invented by John
Milton and first written
into his epic poem, "Para-
dise Lost," a story about
good and evil. Pandemo-
nium is the name of the
devil's city in the poem.
Ever since Milton coined
the term in 1667 to mean
"all demons," it has evolved
to mean any chaotic situ-
ation, even one as cute as
pandas on the loose.

Pollyanna

(*pol-ee-**AN**-uh*), noun or adjective
A person who always looks on
the bright side, no matter what.
Always happy and upbeat.

*That Pollyanna has been standing
outside in the rain for hours
waiting to buy tickets to the
play—and she's still smiling!*

Pop Culture

In the children's novel of the same name, Pollyanna is an orphan who is determined to be positive. After her father passes away, she goes to live with her wealthy but unloving aunt in a sad little town, but Pollyanna ends up spreading happiness there. Whenever something bad happens, she plays a game her father had taught her—to always think of the good in the situation. Pollyanna shares this game with everyone she meets, slowly influencing the entire town and turning it into a joyful place. Now Pollyanna means someone who is sunny and optimistic, no matter how terrible the circumstances. This 1913 novel by Eleanor H. Porter was a bestselling book and has been adapted into multiple movies.

poobah

(**POO**-*bah*), noun

Someone who believes they have great importance— but they really don't.

The Grand Poobah hammered his gavel and called the meeting to order, even though no one was paying attention to him.

Synonym: muckety-muck

Pop Culture

The Grand Pooh-bah is a character from a comic opera called *The Mikado*. He thinks he is extremely important and gives himself all sorts of titles, like "Lord High Admiral" and "Lord High Everything Else." Unfortunately, he is Lord High Nothing and has no authority, so that's where *poobah* gets its meaning. The title "The Grand Poobah" has been used in television too. Cartoon character Fred Flintstone belonged to the Loyal Order of Water Buffaloes, a club whose leader was called "The Grand Poobah."

scaramouche

(**SKAIR**-*uh-moosh*), noun

A person who acts like he's the best ever, but he's really a coward.

That scaramouche talks a big game, but he backs down when you question him.

serendipity

(*ser-uhn-**DIP**-i-tee*), noun

1. A fun, cool discovery made completely by accident.
2. Good luck that comes up unexpectedly.

It was serendipity when the stray dog showed up on our doorstep. (Because now he's our best friend!)

Synonym: kismet

The Roots

In Italian theater, Scaramouche is known as a clown character who first appeared in the 1600s. The word comes from the Italian *scaramuccia*, which literally means "little skirmisher"—someone involved in minor fights. The character often bragged and boasted about himself, causing him to get pummeled by another character for comedic effect, like slapstick comedy.

Pop Culture

Serendipity comes from a Persian fairytale, "The Three Princes of Serendip." (Serendip is a former name for the country Sri Lanka.) Author Horace Walpole was retelling the tale when he used the term "serendipity" to describe the princes' lucky ability to discover wondrous surprises on their adventures. The word was serendipitous (and successful in sticking around). Serendipity is also the name of a famous restaurant and ice cream parlor founded in New York City over fifty years ago, and that has inspired similar restaurants in Chicago, Las Vegas, and other major cities. (Think of all the fabulous flavors you'll find!)

quixotic

(*kwik-SOT-ik*), adjective
Idealistic, unrealistic, impractical.
Even though she wasn't real, Don Quixote loved Dulcinea and went on quests to win her heart—how quixotic!

The Roots

Don Quixote (dahn kee-HO-tay) is the main character of the Spanish novel of the same name, written by author Miguel de Cervantes in the early 1600s. Don Quixote reads so many idealistic adventure stories, he believes himself to be living in one. He pretends to be a knight, mistakes windmills for evil giants, and attacks them. His behavior is ruled by his imagined fantasy world. Therefore, a "quixotic" person is someone who acts or thinks like Don Quixote.

PACHYDERM CHIMERA

MINIMUS WHANGDOODLE

PALOMINO MENAGERIE

BUGBEAR HIPPOCAMPUS

SNALLYGASTER SPHINX

BASILISK HIPPOGRIFF

COCKATRICE FIREDRAKE

FANTASTIC BEASTS

Words for unusual creatures and marvelous monsters—both real and imaginary

On a trip to your local zoo, you're likely to see *pachyderms* (elephants) or a *palomino* pony, but you're not going to find a *chimera*, a *firedrake*, or a *whangdoodle* while you're there. From the monster that used to live under your bed (or is that *bugaboo* still there?), to creatures that heroes fought in great myths and legends (like *hippogriffs* and *sphinxes*), to a few that could actually be someone's pet (hello, *pollywogs* and *mudpuppies*)—here's a collection—a *menagerie*—just for you!

anemone

(*uh-**NEM**-uh-nee*), noun

1. A flowering plant with divided leaves and showy flowers.
2. A bright and colorful marine animal whose
   tentacles look like a flower.

Penelope found a sea anemone washed up in Hawaii and almost added it to her bouquet of flowers because she didn't realize it wasn't a plant.

basilisk

(***BAS**-uh-lisk*), noun

1. A mythical serpent, lizard, or dragon that can
   destroy enemies with just a look.
2. A species of tropical American iguana-like lizard that
   can run across the surface of water on its back legs.

The basilisk always won the staring contests with the other lizards—they couldn't look at him or they'd be destroyed!

bugaboo

(***BUHG**-uh-boo*), noun

1. An imaginary creature that's scary or worrying.
2. Anything that is annoying or causes distress.

My mom says they're not real, but I swear there's a bugaboo in my closet, and it's freaky!

bugbear

(***BUHG**-bair*), noun

1. A frightening creature, like a goblin.
2. Anything you dread or makes you annoyed. A problem.

In order to make children behave, grown-ups sometimes make up stories about bugbears to frighten them.

chimera

(*ki-**MEER**-uh*), noun

1. A fire-breathing female monster from Greek mythology that has the head of a lion, the body of a goat, and a serpent's tail.
2. A dream, a fantasy, an illusion—something that lives on in your imagination.

Open your eyes—there's no chimera there!

cockatrice

(***KOK**-uh-tris*), noun

A monster with the head and wings of a rooster and the body of a dragon.

Having a cockatrice for a pet is not a good idea, unless you're some kind of wizard who can control it!

cryptozoology

(*krip-toh-zoh-**OL**-uh-jee*), noun

The study of unconfirmed creatures like Bigfoot and the Loch Ness Monster.

When I grow up, I want to be a cryptozoologist and capture the chupacabra.

gargoyle

(*GAHR-goil*), noun

A weird-looking, kind of ugly statue of a man or animal on a building. It acts as a spout to carry rainwater away, but is also believed to frighten evil spirits and protect the building.

The gargoyles on the building were carved hundreds of years ago by craftsmen who specialized in that one type of statue.

firedrake

(*FAHY-uhr-dreyk*), noun

A mythical fire-breathing dragon.

Don't wake the firedrake unless you want to be toast for breakfast!

The Roots

A gargoyle at the top of a building is more than just decoration to ward off evil spirits. The French word for gargoyle, *gargouille,* which comes from an Old French term for "throat." Rainwater flows off the roof, into gutters and then through the gargoyle's throat—out and away from the building. This protects the structure from water damage. Speaking of water, when you're sick and your doctor tells you to rinse your throat with salt water, you can tell her that *gargle* also comes from *gargouille.*

hippocampus

(*hip-uh-**KAM**-puhs*), noun

1. A mythological sea creature with the front legs and head of a horse and the tail of a dolphin.
2. An area of the brain responsible for emotion, memory, and the nervous system. Its shape resembles a sea horse.

I wonder why the mermaid is more popular than a hippocampus—a horse-dolphin sea creature is more interesting to me than a woman-fish!

hippogriff

(*__HIP__-uh-grif*), noun

A creature of legend that is half horse and half eagle.

You'd think a hippogriff was half hippopotamus, but instead it's half horse.

hobgoblin

(*__HOB__-gob-lin*), noun

Like a boogeyman—a mischievous goblin or creature that causes fear.

It's easy to be scared of hobgoblins—they can hide anywhere and easily trick you.

leviathan

(*lih-__VAHY__-uh-thuhn*), noun

1. A sea monster.
2. A large sea animal, like a blue whale.
3. Anything ginormous that has incredible power.

The leviathan in the movie was a giant octopus whose arms wrapped around the ship and pulled it under water, sinking it.

menagerie

(*muh-__NAJ__-uh-ree*), noun

A collection of wild animals used for entertainment.

Penelope has a glass menagerie with all kinds of animals, but her favorite is the elephant because his raised trunk sparkles in the sunlight.

minimus

(*MIN-uh-muhs*), noun

1. A creature that is the tiniest or least important.
2. Your pinkie finger or pinkie toe.

The smallest mouse in the house is the minimus.

Level Up!

The plural of *minimus* is *minimi*. Nope, that's not pronounced "mini me"! Instead, it's "mini my."

mudpuppy

(*MUHD-puhp-ee*), noun
Your new dog after a romp in the rain. Kidding! It's a type of salamander.

I have a pet guppy but I really want a mudpuppy. I can keep it in the same glass bowl but without so much green water!

pachyderm

(*PAK-ih-durm*), noun
Originally a classification of a group of mammals that have thick skin and sometimes hooves or nails that look like hooves. Animals like the elephant, hippo, and rhino are all considered pachyderms. Today, each of these animals is classified by more specific features; however, we still refer to them as pachyderms.

When the pachyderms travel together, they don't need to pack trunks—the elephants already have enough!

palomino

(*pal-uh-MEE-noh*), noun
A light-colored horse with a white mane and tail.

The palomino at the farm is named Sky because her light color makes her look like a cloud.

pollywog

(*POL-ee-wog*), noun

A tadpole.

A pollywog turns into a frog. (And then does the frog turn into a prince?)

snallygaster

(*SNAL-ee-gas-ter*), noun

A mythical creature that is part bird, part reptile, and only comes out at night to hunt children and poultry. Originated in rural Maryland.

The snallygaster likes to prey on chickens, so lock up your coop at night!

The Roots

The legend of the snallygaster originated in rural Maryland from German immigrants who spoke of a creature called "Schneller Geist," or "quick spirit." The folklore surrounding this beast goes back to the 1700s Germany, but in the early 1900s, an American newspaper ran a story where locals saw an enormous winged animal with hooks as claws, a sharp beak, and a single eye. The snallygaster reportedly snatched a man and dumped his lifeless body on a hill. Horrifying rumors spread all across the United States, and even President Theodore Roosevelt, a passionate hunter, offered to track down the snallygaster himself. The last sighting occurred in March 1909, when three Maryland men claimed to have fought it off and the creature escaped into the forest. After that, the snallygaster is said to have died, but the folklore around it remained. The snallygaster gave rise to another word—*snollygoster*—which means a sneaky, clever, but dishonest person.

sphinx

(*sfingks*), noun

1. A female creature from Greek mythology with wings and the body of a lion; known for giving people riddles to solve—and killing them if they couldn't answer.
2. An ancient Egyptian form with the head of a man on a lion's body.
3. A person who is like a riddle, or mysterious.

The sphinx was very beautiful, but its wings and lion's body also made it terrifying.

Level Up!

There's a breed of hairless cat with large ears called a Sphynx, pronounced the same way as *sphinx*. So this term can be used for creatures both real and imaginary!

whangdoodle

(**WANG**-dood-l), noun
An imaginary creature.

No one knows what a whangdoodle really looks like, because it lives only in your imagination.

The Roots

Whangdoodle was a British word for a fanciful object whose name was unknown. Authors Roald Dahl and Julie Andrews Edwards borrowed the word, and used it to mean a "fanciful creature." Dahl featured the whangdoodle in three of his stories, *The Minpins*, *James and the Giant Peach*, and *Charlie and the Chocolate Factory*. Actress and singer Julie Andrews (who wrote under her married name, Julie Edwards) wrote *The Last of the Really Great Whangdoodles* about Whangdoodleland, a magical kingdom created by the Whangdoodle for himself and other imaginary creatures, like the Sidewinders and Flukes, to thrive in.

WOEBEGONE FELICITY

BLASÉ UNFLAPPABLE

ZONKED SANGFROID

AGOG CONNIPTION

APOPLECTIC ALOOF

ATINGLE BALLISTIC

CRESTFALLEN OOMPH

ALL THE FEELS

Words to capture the highest of highs and the lowest of lows (and the feelings that are neither)

How are you feeling today? Happy, sad, or angry? Exhausted, bored, or calm? Maybe you're just OK. Or maybe none of those words cut it! You're beyond just being mad—you're *apoplectic*. You're so down, you're *downtrodden*. Everything is so perfect, you can't help but be *ebullient*! Whatever mood you're in, you're going to find the word to describe it here—and they are sure to not leave you *humdrum*, but absolutely thrill you!

agog

(*uh*-**GOG**), adjective or adverb

Eagerly excited and excitedly eager.

The dog was agog waitin' for his bacon—he wouldn't stop jumping and barking in anticipation!

Synonym: impatient

aloof

(*uh*-**LOOF**), adjective or adverb

1. Not interested and not paying attention.
2. Not friendly.

Alfred was aloof when the teacher gave directions, so he didn't know how to do the assignment.

apoplectic

(*ap-uh*-**PLEK**-*tik*), adjective

Extremely angry. Like, red-in-the-face angry.

The moviegoers were apoplectic when the power went off in the middle of the new movie and the theater was refusing to refund any of their money!

Synonym: ballistic

atingle

(*uh*-**TING**-*guhl*), adjective

So excited that you tingle with energy.

Every Christmas Eve, kids all around the world are all atingle awaiting Chris Kringle.

Synonym: thrilled

ballistic

(*buh-**LIS**-tik*), adjective

Suddenly angry or excited, like you are going to explode.

Alfred went absolutely ballistic *when Penelope took his favorite bowling ball without asking. He went* ballistic *again when he bowled a strike anyway.*

Synonym: apoplectic

blasé

(***BLAH-ZEY***), adjective

Bored or unconcerned. BORING!

This sentence is so blasé. *Couldn't you come up with something more exciting?*

cock-a-hoop

(*kok-uh-**HOOP***), adjective

1. Extremely happy and excited—and proud to tell everyone about it.
2. Crooked or off-balance.

Alfred's all cock-a-hoop *about getting a basketball hoop for his driveway—he can't wait to practice day and night.*

Synonyms: akimbo, catawampus, cockeyed

collywobbles

(***KOL**-ee-wob-uhlz*), noun

Dizziness, queasiness or that nervous feeling of butterflies in the stomach.

Being in the class play gave Alfred the collywobbles *on opening night; looking out at the crowd, he felt jittery, as though he might faint.*

Synonym: anxiety

conniption

(*kuh-**NIP**-shuhn*), noun

An outburst of extreme anger.

The class had a conniption *when their teacher took away the candy Penelope brought in to share.*

copacetic

(*koh-puh-SET-ik*), adjective
Totally OK.
*Don't panic about rain ruining the picnic, it's all copacetic.
We'll just spread blankets on the floor and have it inside!*
Synonym: hunky-dory

crestfallen

(*KREST-faw-luhn*), adjective
Greatly disappointed, sad, and discouraged.
Slumping shoulders and drooping head.
*Alfred was crestfallen when Penelope beat him in the
Student Council election. He really wanted to win!*
Synonyms: downtrodden, melancholy

doldrums

(*DOHL-druhmz*), noun
A sad, quiet, downbeat mood.
*Ever since I got a D on
my dinosaur test, I've
been in the doldrums.*

downtrodden

(*DOUN-trod-n*), adjective
When someone is at their
lowest because they've been
walked all over, stepped
on, and pushed around.
*Don't be so downtrodden—
stand up for yourself and
tell that jerk to back off!*
Synonyms: crestfallen,
melancholy

The Roots

In Old English, the word *dol*
means "foolish" and "dull."
It's thought that the "rum"
on the end of *doldrum* is
to pattern it like the word
tantrum. (But no one can
call a toddler tantrum dull,
that's for sure!) "The Doldrums" is one of the places
of The Lands Beyond in the
middle-grade novel, *The
Phantom Tollbooth*. There,
a bunch of lazy people *lollygag* around all day.

druthers

(*DRUHTH-erz*), noun

What you would choose to have, if given a choice.

If they had their druthers, my brothers would eat pepperoni pizza for breakfast, lunch, and dinner. (But mothers don't allow brothers to have their druthers.)

Synonym: preference

Level Up!

The phrase "I'd rather" is pronounced "I'd ruther" in some areas of the U.S. "I'd ruther" got smushed together, dropped the "I" and added an "s" to become *druthers*.

ebullient

(*ih-BUHL-yihnt*), adjective

So thrilled that you feel like you're floating on cloud nine.

Penelope felt ebullient when she got a blue ribbon for her science fair project.

Synonyms: excited, lively

feckless

(*FEK-lis*), adjective

Lacking the ability or energy to do something.

I feel so feckless that I think I should take a nap.

Synonym: lackadaisical, lazy

felicity

(*fi-LIS-i-tee*), noun

1. The state of being incredibly happy.
2. Something that causes happiness.

Volunteering at the animal shelter brings Alfred such felicity, especially since he's not allowed to have a pet 'cause of his mom's allergies.

Synonym: delighted

fiddle-footed

(*FID-l-foot-id*), adjective
Excitable and jittery.
The new puppy became fiddle-footed every time he saw a squirrel—we had to keep a good hold on his leash to make sure he didn't get loose!
Synonym: skittish

flippant

(*FLIP-uhnt*), adjective
Silly or thoughtless about something serious.
Alfred always gets in trouble for his flippant attitude—he got grounded for a week for being disrespectful to his mom.

hangdog

(*HANG-dawg*), adjective
Upset, defeated, or guilty appearance, like a dog that pooped in the house.
Wipe that hangdog look off your face—things will get better!

heartstrings

(*HAHRT-stringz*), noun
Strong, deep, meaningful feelings of love or affection.
My pug's adorable mug tugs on my heartstrings.

The Roots

The word *heartstrings* has its history in medicine. Doctors believed that the heart was controlled by a specific nerve—which they called the heartstring. In the 1500s, the word began to be used figuratively, to mean affection and feelings of love ('cause love *does* tend to control our hearts).

heebie-jeebies

(*HEE-bee-JEE-beez*), noun
Nervous feelings that happen when you are scared or anxious.
The creepy cobwebs of the basement give me the heebie-jeebies. I won't go down there!

ho-hum

(*HOH-huhm*), adjective or interjection
So dull and boring that you can't help yawning.
The soccer game is so ho-hum—nothing exciting has happened in the entire hour and a half!
Synonyms: humdrum

hunky-dory

(*HUHNG-kee-DAWR-ee*), adjective

When everything is good and just right.

No matter how stressed Alfred is, he tells people he's fine and that everything is hunky-dory.

Synonym: copacetic

humdrum

(*HUHM-druhm*), adjective

Boring. Dull. The same old thing—nothing new or exciting.

I couldn't wait to leave that party; there was no music, no food, and it was humdrum.

Synonym: ho-hum

lackadaisical

(*lak-uh-DEY-zi-kuhl*), adjective

1. Not at all interested and thus slow to do something.
2. Lazy, lazy, lazy.

My brother made a lackadaisical effort to cook dinner—he slapped cheese on bread and shoved it in the toaster oven.

Synonym: feckless

melancholy

(*MEL-uhn-kol-ee*), adjective or noun

3. *(adj.)* Sad.
4. *(noun)* A state of sadness or gloominess.

My melancholy collie can't reach his favorite squeaky toy under the couch.

Synonyms: (adj.) downtrodden, crestfallen; (noun) dejection, mournfulness

miffed

(*MIFT*), adjective

UGH! Upset, irritated, or offended.

Alfred was miffed when he missed the bus by ten seconds.

moonstruck

(*MOON-struhk*), adjective

Suddenly obsessed or lost (romantically, mentally, or imaginatively)...as though it were a result of the moon.

Samson was moonstruck over Delilah and was willing to do anything to make her love him—including telling her the secret to defeating him.

oomph

(*oomf*), noun

Energy and excitement. That get-up-and-go feeling.

Alfred always needs a cup of coffee; otherwise, he lacks the oomph he needs to start the morning.

pusillanimous

(*pyoo-suh-LAN-uh-muhs*), adjective

Afraid or cowardly.

The pusillanimous kid runs away from tough situations instead of confronting them.

Synonym: lily-livered, cowardly, gutless

sangfroid

(*sahn-frwa*), noun

The state of being cool and calm, whatever the circumstances.

It's amazing how nothing ever seems to faze Lola—the room could be burning down around her, and she'd still have sangfroid.

Synonym: aplomb

unflappable

(*uhn-FLAP-uh-buhl*), adjective

Not irked by anything, even stuff that bothers everyone else.

The unflappable geese did not move off the road even with all the cars honking.

Synonym: unruffled

verisimilitude

(*ver-uh-si-**MIL**-i-tood*), noun
The state of being similar to reality or the truth. (It sounds like "very similar," doesn't it?)
The story of Pinocchio isn't known for its verisimilitude—noses don't actually grow when you lie!

verklempt

(*fuhr-**KLEMPT***), adjective
So overwhelmed with emotion that you're choked up.
Alfred was verklempt when he saw photos of the cutest puppies up for adoption.
Synonym: speechless

woebegone

(***WOH**-bi-gawn*), adjective
Filled with woe and showing signs of woe. (Whoa, what's *woe*? Troubles or regret.)
I wish my woebegone days would be gone, I'm tired of worrying all the time.

zonked

(*zongkt*), adjective
Worn out, dizzy, tired, exhausted, done, asleep.
I'm feeling zonked so I'll catch some Zs. Zzzzzzzzzz.

zwodder

(*zwod-der*), noun
A state of being extremely tired—so tired that you're woozy, slurring your words, and not able to think straight.
Sometimes when you're zonked, you're in a zwodder and stop making any sense.

Level Up!

Zwodder isn't a well-known word—in fact, it's specific to a small area in England, and you won't find it in American dictionaries. But it's so much fun to say, isn't it? When you say it, you *sound* like you're exhausted! Maybe we should use it in America. (*Psst, pass it on!*)

SPOILSPORT

GENTEEL

FINICKY

INCORRIGIBLE

SKYLARK

CHUTZPAH

ZAFTIG

WHIMSICAL

PERSNICKETY

MOXIE

GONZO

AVUNCULAR

GUMPTION

QUIRKY

IDENTITY CRISIS

Words to describe any personality— from the sweet and kind to the zany or lazy

Writing about someone who is bold and brave? Why not say that they have *moxie* or a lot of *gumption*? Call someone who is super picky about everything *finicky*. Your little sibling is weak or indecisive, so the perfect word to use is *namby-pamby*! Your aunt gives the best hugs because she's pleasantly plump—*zaftig* is the much more pleasing word you need. The world is full of all kinds of personalities and characters, so you're going to need a bunch of adjectives to help you describe the distinctive qualities—let's get started!

anthropomorphic

(*an-thruh-puh-**MAWR**-fik*),
adjective
Giving human qualities to
something that is not human.
*E. B. White was known for writing
about anthropomorphic creatures—
there was Charlotte, the spider who
weaves wonderful words into her
web; Stuart Little, a mouse who
is the youngest child in a family of
humans; and Louie, a mute swan
who learns to play the trumpet.*

avuncular

(*uh-**VUHNG**-kyuh-ler*), adjective
Looking or behaving like
a favorite uncle.
*I wish my Uncle Pete would act
more like my avuncular soccer
coach. Coach Ade is always
helpful and makes sure the
team always has a good time!*

The Roots

In Latin, the word *avunculus*
means "mother's brother,"
and that's where *avuncu-
lar* comes from. Let's just
hope your father's brother
isn't feeling left out!

cantankerous

(*kan-**TANG**-ker-uhs*), adjective
Difficult to get along with or
in a bad mood. Grouchy.
*TV shows and movies love using
cantankerous old men—the
grumpier they are, the funnier
the story gets when the main
character annoys them!*
Synonym: cranky

chutzpah

(***HEUT**-spuh*), noun
You've got a lot of nerve!
Having a lot of guts to do or
say something you maybe
shouldn't, but you do anyway.
*We wanted autographs from
our favorite band, but Penelope
was the only one with enough
chutzpah to sneak backstage.*
Synonyms: guts, moxie, nerve

English Words Borrowed from Yiddish

Yiddish is a German-based language with some Hebrew, Russian, and Polish sprinkled in, usually spoken by people with Jewish roots. Many Jewish Americans remember hearing their "bubbe and zayde" (grandma and grandpa) speak Yiddish, and the language is still spoken today in parts of the United States, Europe, Russia, and Israel. Some words from Yiddish have wiggled their way into English, and are really fun to say...like:

- ► *Chutzpah* (guts, nerve)
- ► *Noodge* (annoying person)
- ► *Nudnik* (dumb, boring person)
- ► *Tchotchke* (little trinket)
- ► *Schlep* (run around from place to place)
- ► *Schmooze* (be social)
- ► *Verklempt* (overwhelmed with emotion)

finicky

(*FIN-i-kee*), adjective
Overly picky or particular—like when someone won't eat the crust of their grilled cheese. When someone is finicky, they are hard to please. (Ooh, that rhymes!)
The finicky feline refused to finish the fish.
Synonym: persnickety

freewheeling

(*FREE-WEE-ling*), adjective
1. Free of rules, regulations, or responsibilities. Carefree.
2. Irresponsible.
Alfred was in a freewheeling mood; with no worries, he got on his bike, going wherever the path took him, for the entire day.
Synonym: happy-go-lucky

genteel

(*jen-TEEL*), adjective
Very polite, sweet, and elegant.
*The genteel grandmother
invited us to a formal tea
in her rose garden and sent
thank-you notes afterwards.*
Synonym: refined

gonzo

(*GON-zoh*), adjective
Wild, weird, and unusual.
*Sam's mom loves to experiment
and create gonzo recipes
like spaghetti tacos—but no
matter how weird, whatever
she makes is always delicious!*
Synonym: quirky, offbeat

gumption

(*GUHMP-shuhn*), noun
The energy and ability to deal with anything and never give up.
*That girl had the gumption to grab the World Record for gum
chewing even though she just lost her two front teeth!*
Synonyms: chutzpah, guts, moxie, nerve

idiosyncrasy

(*id-ee-uh-SING-kruh-see*), noun
An unusual feature or a peculiar way of doing
things that is specific to one person.
Penelope's idiosyncrasy is that she eats gummy worms with a fork.
Synonym: quirk

Pop Culture

Gonzo the Great is a Muppet who made his debut in 1976. He's a daredevil performance artist, inventing wacky stunts, usually accompanied by music, bad poetry, and chickens. (Gonzo's girlfriend is Camilla the chicken.) He may be some kind of bird himself, because he has a long—although crooked—beak, but no one is really sure.

incorrigible

(*in-KAWR-i-juh-buhl*), adjective
When a person cannot be corrected, changed, improved.
That incorrigible kid keeps getting detention—he's late every day!

moxie

(*MOK-see*), noun
1. Courage and daring.
2. Energy and excitement.
3. Skill.

That girl has a lot of moxie to jump on stage and perform uninvited with the rock band.
Synonyms: chutzpah, gumption, guts, nerve

namby-pamby

(*NAM-bee-PAM-bee*),
adjective or noun
1. *(adj.)* Weak or indecisive; lacking character.
2. *(noun)* Someone who can't make a decision—or doesn't want to.

My brother is such a namby-pamby—whenever we go out to eat, he'll order whatever his friends suggest, even if he doesn't like it.
Synonym: (adj.) wishy-washy; (noun) doormat

Pop Culture

Did you know? One of the first soft drinks in America was called Moxie! But the soda was actually invented as a medicine to ease nervousness. Its label read "Moxie Nerve Food." Yep, people bought Moxie because they believed it would give them *oomph*, *pizzazz*, get-up-and-go guts to leave their fears behind. The term *moxie* soon began to describe more than just a beverage…it meant those who were daring, with a lot of nerve. Have you got *moxie*?

persnickety

(*per-SNIK-i-tee*), adjective
Extremely picky.
Alfred is so persnickety, he won't eat anything
that is green, red, or yellow!
Synonym: finicky

poltroon

(*pol-TROON*)
(*noun*) The worst coward you can imagine.
(*adj.*) Completely cowardly.
My brother is such a poltroon—he's scared of everything!
Synonyms: (adj.) lily-livered, pusillanimous; (noun) dastard, milksop

pomposity

(*pom-POS-i-tee*), noun
The state of being pompous (feeling like you're
the greatest person in the world).
My brother's not the boss of me! What pomposity!

quirky

(*KWUR-kee*), adjective
Odd, peculiar, and unusual,
often in a funny way.
Kitty likes to wear cat ears and
a tail everywhere she goes—
she doesn't care if other people
think her habit is quirky!
Synonyms: bizarre, offbeat

scatterbrained

(**SKAT**-er-breynd), noun

Someone who's forgetful, disorganized, and unable to think straight.

When Alfred gets home, he puts his keys down, but he gets scatterbrained and can't remember where!

simpatico

(sim-**PAH**-ti-koh), adjective

Like-minded and likeable; easy to get along with.

The librarian and I are simpatico when it comes to the type of stories we both enjoy.

Synonym: agreeable

skylark

(**SKY**-lahrk), verb

To be playful; to fool around and have fun.

The kids are flying a kite and skylarking on the beach.

Synonym: frolic

spoilsport

(**SPOIL**-spawrt), noun

Someone who spoils all the fun.

Jamie is such a spoilsport—if we don't do things exactly how she wants to, she refuses to participate, or even worse, she tattles.

supercilious

(soo-per-**SIL**-ee-uhs), adjective

Super silly. Just kidding! (Even though that's what it sounds like.) It means feeling superior to other people.

Sofie is so supercilious—she always acts like she's so much better than the rest of us!

Synonyms: arrogant, snotty

vivacious

(*vi-VEY-shuhs*), adjective
Lively and bubbly.
Penelope is vivacious on her birthday, bursting with excitement, nearly floating as she walks!
Synonyms: animated, spirited

venturesome

(*VEN-chur-suhm*), adjective
Willing to take on risk, daring, and danger.
Even though people have died attempting to climb Mt. Everest before, the venturesome duo plans to scale the world's highest mountain next year.
Synonym: courageous

whimsical

(*WIM-zi-kuhl*), adjective
Playful and clever.
Winnie loves to watch baking shows because the flavors, colors, and decorations they use in their creations are often so whimsical!

winsome

(**WIN**-suhm), adjective

Unlike the way the word sounds, this is not when you win something! It's when you are sweet, nice, and charming.

The opposing team thought Alfred was winsome
when he invited them for ice cream.

Synonyms: engaging, pleasant

wishy-washy

(**WISH**-ee-wosh-ee), adjective

1. Going back and forth on decisions; unable to figure things out.
2. Weak and backing down easily.

Alfred can be wishy-washy about his pizza—he can never
decide on pepperoni or meatballs, so he just gets plain.

Synonym: namby-pamby

zaftig

(**ZAHF**-tik), adjective

Pleasingly plump (used only to describe a woman).

My grandmother is zaftig and always wears the most beautiful dresses!

The Roots

Zaftig comes from the German word *saftig*, which means "juicy." That makes sense because a fruit that is juicy is also plump.

RUBBERNECK KILLJOY

LACKEY CURMUDGEON

RUGRAT WHIFFLER

GADFLY MOLLYCODDLE

INTERLOPER GALOOT

NUDNIK DESPERADO

CLODHOPPER FLUNKY

STAY IN CHARACTER

Words to describe who or what a person is — the good, the bad, and the in-between

Let's go beyond personality traits and dive into words that describe *WHAT* someone is. With these words, that cute baby crawling around becomes a *rugrat*. The cranky neighbor who's always yelling when you play on their lawn: a *curmudgeon*. Do you have a friend who is a genius OR supersmart? Then they're an *egghead*. And for that teacher who puts the whole class to sleep...*pedant* is the word you need!

These words can all be the subject of a sentence (this means you could replace someone's name with them). Still not clear? Here's a chart to help you make sense of it!

PERSONALITY TRAIT (DESCRIBES THE SUBJECT)	THE PERSON (IS THE SUBJECT)
If someone is acting...	They might be a...
cantankerous	curmudgeon
finicky, persnickety	fussbudget, smellfungus, gadfly
scatterbrained	flibbertigibbet
supercilious	blowhard, braggart, coxcomb
namby-pamby, wishy-washy	whiffler
with chutzpah	whippersnapper

blowhard

(**BLOH**-hahrd), noun

A person who thinks a lot of himself and lets everyone know it.

Samson is such a blowhard—he's always talking about how good he is in sports, how many A's he got on his report card, and how many girls he's taken on dates!

Synonym: braggadocio

braggadocio

(brag-uh-**DOH**-shee-oh), noun

1. Someone who boasts or brags a lot.
2. The act of bragging or boasting.

The braggadocio thinks he's the most popular kid in the neighborhood and keeps dropping the names of all his so-called friends.

buckaroo

(*buhk-**UH**-roo*), noun

1. A cowboy.
2. Someone who breaks (tames) wild horses so you can ride them with a saddle.

That buckaroo rode the bronco for the full 8 seconds he needed to qualify for the competition.

busybody

(*__BIZ__-ee-bod-ee*), noun

Someone who's always sticking their nose into someone else's business.

The busybody won't stop asking about the party for my sister, who she doesn't even know!

bumpkin

(*__BUHMP__-kin*), noun

An awkward or simple person from a rural area. (They tend not to have a lot of experience in the way the world works!)

Allen felt like a bumpkin on his first trip to New York City because he came from a town with just a hundred people in it.
Synonym: yokel

clodhopper

(*__KLOD__-hop-er*), noun

1. A big, clumsy, often not very smart, person.
2. An awkward, small-town, country person.
3. A large, strong, heavy shoe.

Alfred became a clodhopper when he wore clodhoppers, because they were too big and made him trip all over the place.
Synonyms: bumpkin, yokel

coxcomb

(*KOKS-kohm*), noun
Someone who thinks a
lot of himself and struts
around like a rooster.
*That coxcomb thinks he rules
the schoolyard. He walks around
and tells all the kids what to do
and where they can hang out.*

curmudgeon

(*ker-MUHJ-uhn*), noun
A difficult, cranky person
with a bad temper.
*That curmudgeon belongs in a
dungeon so no one can hear his
complaints, stomping, and yelling.*

denizen

(*DEN-uh-zuhn*), noun
A resident or someone
who spends a lot of time
in a specific place.
*My dad spends a lot of time
watching TV; he's basically
a denizen of the den.*

desperado

(*des-puh-RAH-doh*), noun
An outlaw on the run in the
American "Wild West."
*The sheriff dashed after the
desperado after he recognized the
criminal from a "wanted" poster.*

The Roots

If someone is "desperate,"
they are in despair and will do
almost anything to get out
of the bad situation. That's
where we get the word *desperado*. It's from the 1800s
and originated in the American Southwest, where "desperate" was manipulated
to sound like Spanish, since
both English and Spanish
were spoken there.

egghead

(*EG-hed*), noun
Someone who is book-
smart and brainy.
*Whenever Alfred has a question
about anything, he knows he can
always count on Penelope to have
the answer—she's such an egghead!*

flibbertigibbet

(*FLIB-er-tee-jib-it*), noun
A silly, scatterbrained, dizzy, talkative person.
The flibbertigibbet won't stop telling us how to make homemade slime, even though she doesn't do it right! She forgets an ingredient every time and winds up with mush and muck, not slime.

flunky

(*FLUHNG-kee*), noun
An assistant who does all the little chores no one else wants to do.
Alfred is the drama-club flunky, so he sweeps the stage and puts away the props.
Synonym: lackey

fuddy-duddy

(*FUHD-ee-duhd-ee*), noun
Someone who is old-fashioned or a no-fun stick-in-the-mud.
Don't be a fuddy-duddy; ride the upside-down rollercoaster with me!

funambulist

(*fyoo-NAM-byuh-lis*), noun
A tightrope walker.
I'm kind of like a funambulist because I like walking on slacklines.

fussbudget

(*FUHS-buhj-it*), noun
Someone who fusses over things that are minor or not important.
The fussbudget in the cafeteria organizes the sporks so they're all spork-side-up.

gadfly

(*GAD-flahy*), noun
Someone who annoys others with constant complaints and criticism.
My little brother was such a gadfly over vacation. No matter what we did, he wouldn't stop complaining about how bored he was.
Synonym: smellfungus

galoot

(*guh-LOOT*), noun
An awkward or unusual person.
The big galoot trudged around the garden and trampled all the flowers.
Synonym: lummox, hobbledehoy

hobbledehoy

(*HOB-uhl-dee-hoi*), noun

An awkward, clumsy child or young adult.

Alfred's his feet grew faster than the rest of his body, and he was always tripping over himself like a hobbledehoy.

Synonym: galoot, lummox

interloper

(*IN-ter-loh-per*), noun

1. Someone who interferes with something.
2. Someone who does not belong.

Beezus is annoyed that she has to take her little sister Ramona everywhere she goes. Ramona is an interloper and always messes things up.

killjoy

(*KIL-joi*), noun

Someone who ruins all the fun.

Ramona thinks her big sister Beezus is a killjoy who never lets her have any fun.

kleptomaniac

(*KLEP-tuh-MEY-nee-ak*), noun

Someone who has an urge to steal frequently, even though they don't really need to steal.

That kid who takes bikes and skateboards from the park is a kleptomaniac—not only is he stealing, but he already has a ton of that stuff and just keeps taking more!

lackey

(*LAK-ee*), noun

Someone who does what someone else wants, without question. A "yes man"—someone who says yes to everything. A servant.

Alfred didn't have a lackey, so he had to clean up his room himself.

Synonym: flunky, toady, yea-sayer

majordomo

(*mey-jer-DOH-moh*), noun

1. A servant in charge of an important family's home (like a butler to royalty).
2. Someone who makes arrangements for someone else.

The majordomo scheduled a dinner for the prince and his best mates to attend.

The Roots

Majordomo comes from the Medieval Latin phrase *major domus*, which means "highest official of the household." It was used for servants to royalty. *Major-domo* can now mean anyone who takes care of another person's affairs and events. In modern times, *major-domo* has even been used for an email server. If an email is sent to the major-domo, it automatically gets forwarded to every email address on the majordomo's list—it's an electronic virtual servant!

misanthrope

(*MIS-uhn-throhp*), noun
Someone who dislikes humanity.
If the misanthrope hates being around people so much, maybe he should be the first person to live on Mars.

mollycoddle

(*MOL-ee-kod-l*), noun or verb
1. A person who has been overly pampered and taken care of.
2. To treat someone or something with extreme and unnecessary care and attention.

The mollycoddled man doesn't know how to make his bed. Or do his laundry. Or wash his dishes. Yikes!

moocher

(*MOOCH-er*), noun
1. Someone who borrow things without bringing them back or replacing them.
2. Someone who begs or steals.

Alfred is such a moocher! He is constantly borrowing things from people, but never returns them—he needs to buy his own stuff.

muckety-muck

(*MUHK-eh-tee-MUHK*), noun
An important person—who thinks they are more important than they really are.
The kid reporter thinks he's a muckety-muck, but he doesn't even write for the school paper.
Synonym: blowhard

nudnik

(*NOOD-nik*), noun

1. Someone who is annoying.
2. Someone who's boring.

Penelope dreads family get-togethers because her nudnik cousin Harriet always wants to talk about the most boring things and never leaves Penelope alone.

pedagogue

(*PED-uh-gog*), noun

A dull and boring schoolteacher—they put you to sleep with their lessons!

Will the word "pedagogue" impress your teacher? (Yes, as long as you don't yawn and call her one.)

pettifogger

(*PET-ee-fog-er*), noun

A lawyer whose methods are shady or underhanded. Someone who keeps arguing when their argument is small and silly.

Lawyers who try to twist or hide evidence in order to win their chase are nothing but a bunch of pettifoggers.

The Roots

As far as we know, *pettifogger* initially started out as two words: *petty*, which comes from the French word *petite*, or "small," and *fogger*, an obscure old English or German word coming from a family of German merchants whose last name was Fugger. They were known for being bit shady, which is how they gained their wealth. In English, the two words were initially used to describe someone who owned small businesses and made their money in dishonest ways. How the word came to be used specifically for lawyers, is unclear—but the underhanded undertones persist.

ragamuffin

(*RAG-uh-muhf-in*), noun

Someone in tattered clothing who's messy and unkempt.

My little sister is a ragamuffin with her torn pants and skinned knees.

Synonym: tatterdemalion

rainmaker

(*REYN-mey-ker*), noun

1. Someone who causes rain, either by a spell, ritual dance or scientific method.
2. A person who helps their company or business make a lot of money.

The rain forest doesn't need a rainmaker—it's soaking wet already, thanks.

rubberneck

(*RUHB-er-nek*), noun or verb

1. *(noun)* A very curious person.
2. *(verb)* To look at something so interesting, your neck turns to rubber turning around to keep staring at it.

The parents rubberneck their way through school, looking at all our work on the walls.

rugrat

(*RUHG-rat*), noun

Any baby, toddler or young child.

The moms and their rugrats took over the playground— there were toddlers everywhere, so we couldn't play tag or we might step on them!

Level Up!

In business, a rainmaker is someone who gains so many new customers, it's like it is raining money! The rainmaker is so good at their job, their success appears as if by magic.

Pop Culture

Remember that kid TV channel Nickelodeon? It had an awesome show called *The Rugrats*, which was a cartoon featuring babies and toddlers. It made its debut in 1991 and ran on and off for thirteen years (it was popular enough to even get a spin-off show that featured the characters in elementary and middle school, called *All Grown Up*). The main rugrat was Tommy, who came from a Jewish family, so some episodes centered on Jewish culture, like the holidays of Passover and Hanukkah.

smellfungus

(*smel-**FUHNG**-guhs*), noun

Someone who finds fault in everything and is impossible to please.

Nothing Alfred does can make Penelope happy—she's such a smellfungus!

Synonym: gadfly

tatterdemalion

(*tat-er-di-**MEYL**-yuhn*), adjective or noun

1. *(noun)* Someone dressed in tattered clothing or rags.
2. *(adj.)* Messy, dirty, and falling apart.

Sew up that split in your pants if you don't want to be a tatterdemalion.

Synonym: ragamuffin

tub-thumper

(***TUHB**-thuhm-per*), noun

A loud and intense supporter of a specific cause.

Alese is a tub-thumper when it comes to treating pit bulls with kindness—she has adopted two of them and is quick to defend them when people say they are dangerous.

ultracrepidarian

(*uhl-truh-krep-i-**DAIR**-ee-uhn*), adjective or noun

Someone who judges and gives advice outside their area of knowledge.

Penelope is such a know-it-all and is ultra-annoying, but lately she's been ultra-wrong and is proving to be an ultracrepidarian.

wallflower

(***WAWL**-flahw-er*), noun

An extremely shy person who leans against the wall at parties.

The wallflower walked away when asked to waltz.
(In his defense, nobody waltzes anymore!)

Synonym: introvert

whiffler

(***WIF**-ler*), noun

A person who changes their mind...a lot.

Alfred is such a whiffler—first he wanted ice-cream for dessert, then he wanted cake, then he wanted pie, then he wanted ice cream again!

whippersnapper

(***WIP**-er-snap-er*), noun

A young person who insists he is ready for something but he is most definitely NOT.

That whippersnapper will get whipped around riding that bucking bronco!

yea-sayer

(***YEY**-sey-er*), noun

1. Someone who always looks on the bright side.
2. Someone who always says "yes" and lets other people walk all over them.

My sister is a yea-sayer—she always able to find something positive about even the worst situations.

SYNESTHESIA

GLABELLA

NOGGIN

RHINOTILLEXIS

PHILTRUM

ZOONOSIS

UVULA

HORRIPILATION

BURNSIDES

LUNULA

PHLEGM

MUCOPHAGY

CANOODLE

BUCCULA

BODY LANGUAGE

Words for random body parts and curious sensations from head to toe

When you were little, you probably sang, "head, shoulders, knees, and toes, knees and toes," a bunch of times. But that song didn't teach you about your *buccula*, *glabella*, or *uvula*, did it? (Not as catchy, and a bit too hard for preschoolers.) And you may not have facial hair just yet, but just wait till puberty and you might find yourself interested in *pogonotrophy*. From new words for fingerprints, goosebumps, dizziness, and more—you're sure to give this section two ~~thumbs~~ *pollexes* up!

akimbo

(*uh-**KIM**-boh*), adjective or adverb

1. Hands on your hips, with your elbows pointing out.
2. In a bent position.
3. Having any of your limbs flung out widely or chaotically.

Jack stood with his arms akimbo, hoping to show the giant that he wasn't intimidated.

buccula

(***BUHK**-yuh-luh*), noun

A roll of fat under the chin; a double chin.

My grandma poses for photos with her head resting on her chin, hoping to hide her buccula.

burnsides

(***BURN**-sahydz*), noun

A type of beard with whiskers everywhere except on the chin.

My hipster uncle had an awesome beard, but then he shaved just his chin and now he has burnsides.

The Roots

Burnsides are named after American Civil War General Ambrose Burnside, who wore the unusual beard style—a mustache connecting two large bearded areas on the cheeks, but with a cleanly shaven chin. The word *sideburns* came about by doing a bit of a switcheroo from *burnsides*. Now if someone is sporting burnsides, it will most likely be called "mutton-chops" instead (because their shape looks like the cut of meat). And, if you think burnsides are scary-looking, you might have a case of *pogonophobia*, or the irrational fear of beards.

BURNSIDES

GOATEE

MUTTON CHOPS

HANDLEBAR

SHORT BOXED

canoodle

(*kuh-**NOOD**-l*), verb

To cuddle and kiss.

Alfred and Penelope got caught canoodling in the hallway, so the principal gave them detention for breaking the No PDA rule!

dactylogram

(*dak-**TIL**-uh-gram*), noun

A fingerprint.

I know you ate my chocolate. You left sticky dactylograms all over the kitchen!

glabella

(*gluh-**BEL**-uh*), noun

The area between your eyebrows.

Even if you cross your eyes, it's almost impossible to see if your glabella is sprouting a unibrow, unless you look in a mirror.

Odd Body Words

Glabella isn't the only odd name for our odd body parts! Here's a list of a few others:

- ► Cerumen: the technical word for earwax
- ► Columella: the tissue, or skin, at the bottom of your nose that separates your nostrils
- ► Diastema: a gap in your teeth (usually between the two in front)
- ► Orpryon: the part of your forehead that's right above your eye sockets or eyebrows
- ► Purlicue: the space between your thumb and pointer finger
- ► Rasceta: the creases of skin on the palm-side of your wrist
- ► Tragus: the little flap in front of the opening to your ear

hippocampus

(*hip-uh-KAM-puhs*), noun

1. An area of the brain responsible for emotion, memory, and the nervous system. Its shape resembles a sea horse.
2. A mythological sea creature with the front legs and head of a horse and the tail of a dolphin.

People used to have their friends' numbers stored in their hippocampus, but now that everyone has smartphones, they can't remember any of them!

horripilation

(*haw-rip-uh-LEY-shuhn*), noun

Goosebumps.

The Halloween haunted house horrified me and my skin broke out in horripilation.

lunula

(*LOO-nyuh-luh*), noun

The pale half-moon shape at the base of your fingernail.

You can't see Penelope's lunula because she got a manicure with black polish.

minimus

(*MIN-uh-muhs*), noun

1. Your pinkie finger or pinkie toe.
2. A creature that is the tiniest or least important.

When Penelope and her friends have fancy tea parties, they each hold up their minimus when drinking from their cups.

The Roots

The Latin word *luna* means "moon," and *-ula* is a Latin suffix for things that are small. Put them together, and *lunula* means "little moon." So technically, anything with a crescent or half-moon shape can be called a *lunula*—and that includes punctuation. (Yep, a single parenthesis symbol is a *lunula* too!)

mucophagy

(*mew-KOF-uh-gee*), noun
Eating your snot right after you just picked your nose. Gross!
Alfred grosses everyone out with his mucophagy—he constantly sticks his finger in his nose and eats the boogers!

noggin

(*NOG-uhn*), noun
Another word for your head or brain.
There should be laws that force people to wear helmets when skateboarding or riding a bike— you need to protect your noggin!

Pop Culture

Like Nickelodeon, Noggin was a television network for children. It's now a streaming service and features popular shows like *Dora the Explorer*, *Peppa Pig*, and *Paw Patrol* for pre-school kids.

phlegm

(*flem*), noun
The slimy stuff that runs from your nose when you're sick.
I hate having a cold—I can't breathe out of my nose because of all the phlegm blocking it!

philtrum

(*FIL-truhm*), noun
The little indentation on your face between the upper lip and nose.
Penelope's four-year-old sister likes to lick the snot off her philtrum instead of just using tissue like a normal person.

pogonotrophy

(*poh-goh-noh-TROH-fee*), noun
The growing and grooming of a beard, mustache, and other kinds of facial hair.
Alfred stares in the mirror and dreams of shaving and spending his mornings occupied by pogonotrophy.

pollex

(*POL-eks*), noun
Another word for thumb.
Hitchhikers put out a pollex in order to let people know they need a ride.

rhinotillexis

(*RAI*-nuh-til-*EKS*-is), noun
The act of picking your nose with your finger.
When my brother was little, he would wipe his boogers on his shirt after he performed a thorough rhinotillexis.

synesthesia

(*sin-uhs-THEE-zhuh*), noun
When one of the five senses (sight, sound, smell, touch, taste) reacts to something meant for another sense.
A person with synesthesia may say, "That song looks green." (What?!)

Level Up!

There are various kinds of synesthesia because we have five senses, and any combination of them might get mixed up. According to a doctor who studies the disorder, there are about eighty different types of synesthesia. A person with "chromesthesia" sees colors when music is played. When a certain sound causes a negative emotion like anger, it's called "misophonia." With "grapheme-color synesthesia," the most common type, letters, and numbers appear in different colors. Interestingly, many people with this form of synesthesia report the letter A as being red.

uvula

(*YOO-vyuh-luh*), noun
That funny thing that hangs down from the back of your throat.
The doctor always asks you to "Open wide!" so she can see your uvula.

Level Up!

Did you know that when a person snores, the sound can be made by the uvula flapping in the breeze? When the snoring is so loud that it keeps everyone up all night, it might be time to let the snorer know they can have an uvulectomy to remove it. (It's not as painful as the sounds of midnight snores!)

vertigo

(*VUR-tih-goh*), noun
A dizzy feeling like you're spinning around but you're actually still.
When you get off the upside-down rollercoaster, you may have vertigo and feel like you're still going loop-de-loop.

zoonosis

(*zoh-ON-uh-sis*), noun
Any illness or disease that can be passed from animals to humans.
Hand, foot, and mouth disease is a zoonosis that people get from cattle, pigs, sheep, and other animals with split hooves.

SKEDADDLE

SCHLEP

TOOTLE

SCURRYFUNGE

SKIDDOO

VAMOOSE

JIRBLE

FANDANGO

TELEKINESIS

FILLIP

DAWDLE

JITTERBUG

FOOTLOOSE

SASHAY

SPRING INTO ACTION

Words to describe motions and maneuvers

If you love to dance and have sweet moves, you should check out the *fandango*! You're in a hurry, so you're moving fast, *hotfooting* to your next destination, but you have to slow down because someone's moving *so* slowly in front of you—you wish they'd stop *dawdling*. Right before you jump out of bed each morning, you might stretch your arms as far as you can and let out a great big yawn—did you know that movement is called *pandiculation*? There are so many fun words to describe things moving—let's get to them!

dawdle

(*DAWD-l*), verb

To waste so much time while doing something that you end up doing it really slowly.

Don't dawdle while baking doughnuts—I'm hungry and can't wait!

Synonyms: dillydally, footle, lollygag

dillydally

(*DIL-ee-dal-ee*), verb

To drag or linger, and ultimately waste time.

Alfred dillydallied on his walk, kicking a rock and following it wherever it rolled.

Level Up!

The word *dilly* is a slang word we don't hear too much anymore—it means "delightful" and "delicious." But word experts claim "*dillydally*" is a fun reduplication of the word *dally*—not *dilly*—because *dally* means "to act playfully and waste time." Its first use goes all the way back to 1741! It probably could go either way, because if you think about it, aren't you always having a *delightfully* good time when someone tells you to stop dillydallying?

fandango

(*fan-DANG-goh*), noun

1. A fast Spanish-American dance with a man and woman.
2. A dance or a ball, especially in the Southwest U.S.

You can dance and show off your fancy footwork at the fandango— just don't trip over your own feet!

fillip

(*FIL-uhp*), verb

To flick something, typically your finger held back by your thumb.

Alfred is the best paper football player. He knows how to fillip the paper triangle in just the right way to always get it through his opponent's fingers.

footloose

(*FOOT-loos*), adjective

Free to move about and wander because you have no ties to a place or thing.

Sometimes you just want to cut loose and be footloose—just make sure your shoes aren't loose.

Synonyms: unrestrained, free, loose

hobnob

(*HOB-nob*), verb

To mix and mingle with people who are more important than you. (Probably 'cause you're looking to move into the cool crowd too!)

Penelope loved to hobnob with the teachers at school—it made her feel really cool, and she hoped one day she'd be able to be one herself!

Synonym: schmooze

Pop Culture

Footloose is the title of a 1984 movie (there's also a 2011 remake) about a boy named Ren McCormack, who moves from the big city of Chicago to a small town where rock 'n' roll music and dancing have been banned! Ren loves music and dancing, so when the senior prom approaches, he convinces his new friends to rebel against the town's law. The title of the movie not only suggests that Ren and his friends are straying from what's expected, but it also hints that they'll move about freely while dancing!

hotfoot

(*HOT-foot*), adverb or verb

To walk or run in a hurry.

Alfred hotfooted it to the theater so he wouldn't be late for the movie.

jettison

(*JET-uh-suhn*), verb

1. To toss something off a boat or plane, to lighten the load.
2. To throw something away or cast it aside.

Don't jettison the parachute off the jet! We might need it!

Synonym: heave-ho

jirble

(*JUR-buhl*), verb

To accidentally spill something by shaking or pouring with unsteady movement.

I jirbled my juice and more was on the floor than left in my glass.

jitterbug

(*JIT-er-buhg*), noun

1. A bug that gives you the jitters! (Sorry, that's wrong.) It's an energetic dance with acrobatic moves, flips, twirls, and splits.
2. A person who performs the dance.

Penelope has lots of energy and a fearless attitude, and she is a pretty good gymnast, which is why she's great at dancing the jitterbug.

Pop Culture

The jitterbug became popular in the 1940s, performed to the fast-paced music known as "swing" and "boogie-woogie." The jazz singer Cab Calloway recorded a song "The Call of the Jitter Bug" in 1934, which helped make the term popular. The dance is still performed today in jitterbug dance contests all over America.

landslide

(*LAND-slahyd*), noun

1. Rock, soil, and earth that tumble down a steep slope.
2. When someone wins something by a large, or enormous, amount.

Alfred almost caused a landslide *when he began yodeling loudly in the mountains—luckily Penelope stopped him once she noticed some rocks coming loose.*

pandiculation

(*pan-DIK-yuh-LEY-shuhn*), noun

The act of yawning and stretching at the same time.

Zoo visitors gather to watch the pandas' pandiculation *when they wake up. It's cute when they reach their paws into the air.*

rejigger

(*ree-JIG-er*), verb

To change or rearrange something in order to fix something *again*.

Alfred constantly had to rejigger *the lock on the bathroom door—otherwise his sister could accidentally walk in on him!*

sashay

(*sa-SHEY*), verb

To walk or skip while swinging the hips in a happy and confident way.

We sashayed *to the snack machine, excited to pick out treats with the change swishing in our pockets.*

schlep

(*shlep*), verb

To travel or to carry something around—and it's a pain in the neck.

First I had to schlep *to school, and then swim practice, then the student council meeting...PHEW!*

scurryfunge

(*skur-ee-FUHNJ*), verb

To run around cleaning before visitors arrive.

I don't bother to scurryfunge when my friends come over—their rooms are a mess too!

skedaddle

(*skih-DAD-l*), verb

To leave in a hurry.

I can never pet the bunny that lives in my backyard, because each time she sees me coming, she skedaddles away.

skiddoo

(*skih-DOO*), verb

To leave, to get out—quickly!

We'd better skidoo if we want to make it to the movie on time—it starts in five minutes!

somnambulate

(*som-NAM-byuh-leyt*), verb

To sleepwalk.

My dad will sometimes somnambulate in the middle of the night, go to the kitchen, and eat all the cookies.

telekinesis

(*tel-i-ki-NEE-sis*), noun

The ability to move things with your mind.

I wish I could use telekinesis to get my brother out of my room.

teeter-totter

(*TEE-ter-tot-er*), noun or verb
Another name for a seesaw (where you go up and down in alternating movements).
An elephant and a mouse can't ride the teeter-totter together. (The mouse would go flying!)

tootle

(*TOOT-l*), verb
To move or drive in a slow, leisurely way.
Your pet turtle just tootles along like he's got a lifetime to get to where he's going.

vamoose

(*vuh-MOOS*), verb
To leave in a hurry.
Alfred heard there was a mad moose on the loose, so he vamoosed!

whirligig

(*WUR-li-gig*), noun
1. Anything that spins around.
2. A merry-go-round.
3. A dizzy, silly person.

My sister loves to wear slippery socks so she can spin like a whirligig on the kitchen floor. (And then she becomes a whirligiggly!)

The Roots

Vamoose comes from the Spanish *vamos* which means "let us go." The word galloped into English from the American Southwest, where English-speaking and Spanish-speaking cowboys often mingled. They would regularly use each other's words and, of course, mispronounce them. That's how *vamos* got roped into being *vamoose*.

SPAGHETTIFICATION

ZENITH

QUICKSILVER

ROCKOON

EXOPLANET

EXTRATERRESTRIAL

ASTROBLEME

SYZYGY

ASTERISM

GYROSCOPE

PLANETESIMAL

OUT OF THIS WORLD

Words for all things interstellar or astronomical

Space may be the final frontier, but science has proven that the universe is constantly expanding. If you've ever looked up at the stars at night, or been lucky enough to do it through a telescope, you've probably wondered about what else is out there. Are there aliens, or *extraterrestrials*, living in far off *exoplanets*? Before planets became planets, what were they called? There is so much that astronomers and astronauts know, and some of the same discoveries await you...

asterism

(*AS-tuh-riz-uhm*), noun
A recognizable pattern of stars that isn't a whole constellation, like the Big Dipper (which is part of the Constellation Ursa Major, or the Great Bear).
The only part of the constellation Orion I know is the three-star asterism of his belt.

astrobleme

(*AS-truh-bleem*), noun
A mark on the Earth left by an ancient asteroid or meteorite.
Blame the meteorite for the astrobleme.

exoplanet

(*EK-soh-plan-it*), noun
A planet outside our own solar system.
All of the planets that orbit around our sun are so different, but scientists are searching for an exoplanet that has similar temperature and atmosphere to Earth.

Level Up!

For an exoplanet to sustain human life, it needs to meet a lot of specific conditions— like get warmth and light from a nearby star and have liquid water on its surface. It should also be close enough for humans to reach! But the nearest livable exoplanet, Proxima Centauri b, would take you over four years to reach... if you were traveling at the speed of light (which we haven't figured out how to do).

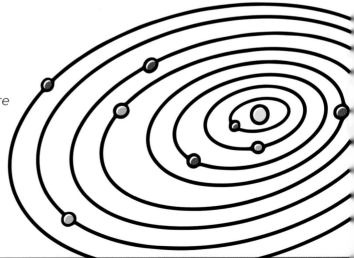

extraterrestrial

(*ek-struh-tuh-RES-tree-uhl*), adjective or noun

1. An alien being from outer space.
2. Anything that comes from outside Earth, beyond its atmosphere.

I hope an extraterrestrial lands in my backyard and becomes my extra-besttrial. (That's a bestie from outer space.)

gyroscope

(*JAI-ruh-skohp*), noun

A gizmo that rotates easily in many different directions, first used to demonstrate the Earth's rotation.

There's a new game show that challenges contestants to answer trivia while rotating in a gyroscope. It not only spins your body around, but it scrambles your brain too!

Pop Culture

In 1982, the summer blockbuster—in fact, the biggest movie of the year—was *E.T.: The Extraterrestrial.* It's all about an alien who gets stranded on Earth, and a boy named Elliot who finds him and tries to help E.T. call home.

In an early scene, Elliot lures E.T. into his home with a trail of Reese's Pieces candy. Based on the original script, the treats were supposed to be M&M's, but the chocolate company turned down the opportunity to appear in the film. At that time, Reese's Pieces were new to the market and not well known, but their cameo in *E.T.* soon made the bite-size peanut butter candies a household name.

planetesimal

(*plan-i-**TES**-uh-muhl*), noun
A tiny pre-planet—they are
the rocks and celestial bodies
(like asteroids) in space
that collide together and
eventually form planets.
*I like to imagine what planets
we've yet to discover, or the
ones that will one day exist, as
planetesimals smash together
and create new ones.*

quicksilver

(***KWIK**-sil-ver*), noun
Another name for mercury,
the element in a thermometer,
which has a silvery look.
*Alfred watched the quicksilver
rise in his thermometer, indicating
that he had a pretty high fever.*

Level Up!

Hold on...what's a chem-
istry word doing in the
astronomy section?

Quicksilver, or mercury,
is one of the elements on
the periodic table, but it's
also the name of one of the
eight planets in our solar
system—the one closest to
the sun.

Mercury was the Roman
god of trade, travel,
schemes, and theft, who
also served as the messen-
ger to all the other gods.
The planet was named
after Mercury because it's
the fastest planet in its
travels around the sun.

Quicksilver, or the ele-
ment of mercury, was
named after the planet
because of its shiny, *fast-
moving* liquid form. It was
used in old-fashioned ther-
mometers because of its
fast reaction to tempera-
ture changes.

rockoon

(*ROK-oon*), noun

A balloon that carries a rocket to a high-altitude
launch. A mash-up of "rocket" and "balloon."

*Before we launch our rocket, we need to create
a rockoon to get it to a higher altitude.*

spaghettification

(*spuh-GET-uh-fuh-KAY-shun*), noun

A theory that the extreme gravity in a black hole
stretches matter into thin strands, like spaghetti,
right before the matter is utterly destroyed.

*Too much gravity creates spaghettification—good thing the gravity
on Earth is just right, 'cause I'd hate to be stretched that thin!*

syzygy

(*SIZ-i-jee*), noun

In astronomy, when at least three objects
in space are in a straight line.

*Whenever there is a solar or lunar eclipse, it's because
the Earth, moon, and sun are in syzygy—they are lined
up perfectly and create the coolest sight.*

zenith

(*ZEE-nith*), noun

1. The part of the sky that's right over your head.
2. The most successful time—the highest point or peak.

*I've never seen the moon in my zenith—it always
seems to be following right behind me!*

SHENANIGANS

MALARKEY

FINAGLE

HONEYFUGGLE

CHARLATAN

HOODWINK

BOGUS

BAMBOOZLE

TARADIDDLE

OUTFOX

CHICANERY

CROCODILIAN

SKULDUGGERY

FLIMFLAM

STRETCHING THE TRUTH

Words for fibbing, twisting, and tricking

If you love to prank your friends on April Fools' Day, don't just trick them—*bamboozle* and *hoodwink* them! You can be clever and *outfox* everyone with this group of words for sneaky practical jokes, tiny white lies, and random *monkeyshines*. But beware! Don't get fooled by someone else's *shenanigans*!

bamboozle

(*bam-BOO-zuhl*), verb
To trick, fool, or confuse.
My brother tried to bamboozle me into thinking our parents had gone on vacation, but they were just at the mall all day,
Synonyms: trick, finagle, flimflam, honeyfuggle, hoodwink, hornswoggle

bogus

(*BOH-guhs*), adjective
Something fake or counterfeit.
I found a bogus five-dollar bill on the boardwalk.

charlatan

(*SHAHR-luh-tin*), noun
A person who claims to have a specific skill but actually has none. A fraud or phony.
The charlatan sold Alfred special bubble gum that was supposed to make him run faster, but he's still the slowest kid on the basketball team!
Synonym: snollygoster

Pop Culture

Jelly Belly® is a pretty tricky company—they sell a game that features jelly-bean pairs that look exactly alike, but each bean in the pair has *wildly* different flavors. One is outrageously delicious, and the other is outrageously disgusting! You may think you're about to eat a chocolate pudding jellybean, but instead, you chomp down on *canned dog food*. How about wanting to munch on a popcorn jellybean, only to realize you've gotten a *rotten egg*? Eww. Gross!

The name of the game is Beanboozled® and it comes from a play on the word *bamboozled*, which means to trick. There are many disgusting flavors in Beanboozled®, like skunk spray, booger, and even barf. You might be rewarded with a strawberry-banana smoothie...or be fooled with a dead fish. Do you dare to try?

chicanery

(*shi-**KAY**-nuh-ree*), noun
Clever, planned trickery.
I think the older kids are up to some kind of chicanery, because they keep whispering, giggling, and looking over here!

Level Up!

In a high-speed car race, a *chicane* is a tight, zigzag part of the course that interrupts a straightaway. It is tricky, causing a driver to steer back and forth quickly. Someone who practices chicanery is crooked, just like the chicane in the road. You have to maneuver quickly around them!

crocodilian

(*krok-uh-**DIL**-ee-uhn*), adjective
Insincere and dishonest.
Like a crocodile.
The crocodilian dragon had a long snout and razor-sharp teeth. Its smile was also crocodilian, since we knew it did not want to be friends—it wanted to eat us!

finagle

(*fi-**NEY**-guhl*), verb
To arrange; to obtain something in a dishonest way.
Don't let him finagle you into trading your best Pokémon card for one that's worthless!
Synonyms: bamboozle, flimflam, honeyfuggle, hoodwink, hornswoggle

flimflam

(***FLIM**-flam*), verb or noun
1. *(verb)* To cheat someone out of money or belongings by trickery.
2. *(noun)* The trick itself.
We asked for change for our ten-dollar bill, but the salesman said we only gave him five—what a load of flimflam!
Synonyms: bamboozle, finagle, honeyfuggle, hoodwink, hornswoggle

honeyfuggle

(***HUHN**-ee-fuh-guhl*), verb
To cheat or swindle.
Don't let anyone honeyfuggle you out of your allowance—you earned that money, and you need to hold onto it!
Synonyms: bamboozle, finagle, flimflam, hoodwink, hornswoggle

hoodwink

(*HOOD*-wingk), verb

To trick or fool.

I got hoodwinked at the Halloween party because everyone was wearing masks and pretending to be someone else!

Synonyms: bamboozle, finagle, flimflam, honeyfuggle, hornswoggle

hornswoggle

(*HAWRN*-swog-uhl), verb

To get the best of someone by cheating them.

That kid hornswoggled me—I paid him fifty cents for a lemonade that was mostly water!

Synonyms: bamboozle, finagle, flimflam, honeyfuggle, hoodwink

humbuggery

(*HUHM*-buhg-uh-ree), noun

Something that is not what it's supposed to be—a fraud, hoax, or sham.

I tried to pretend my dog's medicine was a treat, but he caught on to my humbuggery and wouldn't eat it!

Synonym: skulduggery

malarkey

(*muh-LAHR*-kee), noun

Something that isn't true, is meant to fool you, or is just a lot of nonsense.

I signed up for the Forensics Club thinking we would be solving crimes like detectives, but it's such malarkey that Forensics also means debating! Now I have to do public speaking.

mealymouthed

(*MEE*-lee-moutht), adjective

Saying something that is not sincere or truthful in order to be sneaky and devious.

That kid can be so mealymouthed, no one should ever believe what he says!

monkeyshines

(*MUHNG*-kee-shahynz), noun

Sneaky pranks you pull on someone—also known as monkey business.

My brother thinks his monkeyshines of hiding the TV remote are brilliant, but I just go stream shows on my computer instead.

Synonym: shenanigans

outfox

(*owt-FOKS*), verb
To be more clever than someone else; to outsmart them.
The sheep outfoxed the fox by pretending to be rocks.

pennyweighter

(*PEN-ee-weyt-r*), noun
A thief who steals something expensive by replacing it with a fake, worthless item.
The pennyweighter swiped the pearls and left plastic beads behind.

shenanigans

(*shuh-NAN-i-guhnz*), noun
Pranks, tricks, and mischief.
April Fool's Day is a perfect time for a bunch of shenanigans— it's fun to try and trick as many people as you can!

skulduggery

(*skuhl-DUHG-uh-ree*), noun
Dishonest, tricky, or mean behavior.
Hoping to keep the treasure all to themselves, the kids used a touch of skulduggery to throw everyone else off the trail.
Synonym: subterfuge

taradiddle

(*tar-uh-DID-l*), noun
A tiny lie or fib.
Hoping to impress her friends, Tara told a taradiddle about being able to play the fiddle— but it was really her twin sister Sara who could play.

ABOMINABLE FRENEMY

HOTBED MACHINATIONS

HOODLUM FIREBRAND

TOADY COMEUPPANCE

DIABOLICAL USURP

NEMESIS RAPSCALLION

GUETAPENS MIASMA

THE BAD GUY

Words for villains and troublemakers—and all their evil plans and shady schemes

When a villain plans to kidnap helpless puppies, his *diabolical machinations* must be foiled! His sidekick *toady* may convince a group of no-good *riffraff* to help pull it off, but don't worry, every schemer eventually gets caught and punished—they'll get their *comeuppance*. If you want to steer clear of evil plots, you would be wise to call the words in this section *abominable*!

abominable
(*uh-**BOM**-uh-nuh-buhl*), adjective
Unpleasant, disgusting, to be avoided at all costs!
Some people call Yetis abominable snowmen because they are terrifying. I hope to never meet one!

The Roots

If you look at the word *abominable*, you will notice "omin" hiding in the middle, or as it's known in modern English, "omen." An *omen* is a warning of a future event, usually something bad or evil. The prefix *ab-* in Latin means "away from." Put those together, and the word means to escape from impending doom! *Ahhhhhh!*

comeuppance
(*kuhm-**UHP**-uhnce*), noun
A deserved misfortune that happens to someone who has misbehaved.
The bully got his comeuppance when the kids banded together and shouted him out of the playground. He turned, ran, and tripped!

diabolical
(*dahy-uh-**BOL**-i-kuhl*), adjective
Evil or devilish.
The superhero needed to stop the diabolical scientist from poisoning the city's water supply.

firebrand
(*FAI-yur-brand*), noun
One who stirs up problems—a troublemaker.
When we look back in history, we find many people who were once labeled firebrands, but are now celebrated as heroes for their rebellion.

frenemy

(**FREN**-*uh-mee*), noun
A friend who can be
like an enemy.

*Penelope and Alfred have
been best friends since they
were kids, but lately they've
started fighting all the time—
they have become* frenemies!

Pop Culture

The word *frenemy* didn't
appear in the Merriam-
Webster dictionary until
2009, but the word has
actually been around
since 1953! Journalist
Walter Winchell coined it
to describe the relation-
ship between America and
the Soviet Union during
the Cold War. It took over
fifty years for this word to
become popular.

guetapens

(*get-uh-***PAHN**), noun
An ambush or trap.

*My plan to catch the leprechaun
is to lure him to the* guetapens
with fake gold coins.

Level Up!

Spelling *guetapens* won
Snigdha Nandipati the
Scripps National Spelling
Bee in 2012. Another word
in this book, *logorrhea*,
was also spelled correctly
by Snigdha Nandipati and
won her the 1999 Bee.

Wild Bee Word Winners

Although the word has been used since the late 1800s, no one is sure why spelling bees are called bees. Scripps, the official sponsor of the National Spelling Bee, says it has nothing to do with the insect. Spellers who make it to the national competition are at the top of their game when it comes to words, and to win, they can't afford to make any mistakes! The very first Scripps National Spelling Bee was held in 1925, and the word *gladiolus* (a type of plant in the iris family) won the eleven-year-old his title of champion. Here are some of the winner words from the last few years:

2018: *koinonia* (Christian fellowship/community)

2017: *morocain* (morocco red)

*2016: *Feldenkrais* (a way of moving that eases tension), *gesellschaft* (a very mechanical relationship between people)

*2015: *nunatak* (an Inuit word for a glacial island), *scherenschnitte* (art of paper cutting)

*2014: *feuilleton* (part of a European newspaper or magazine), *stichomythia* (dialogue between two actors)

2013: *knaidel* (a type of dumpling eaten by Jewish people during Passover)

2012: *guetapens* (it's already been defined for you in this book, silly!)

2011: *cymotrichous* (having wavy hair)

2010: *stromuhr* (tool used to measure the amount and speed of blood flow)

*These years had two winners, hence the two words. Before 2014, the last time there were two winners was in 1962, with just one word—**esquamulose** (having smooth skin, not covered in scales).

hoodlum

(*HOOD-luhm*), noun

Someone who is up to no good.

Old people always seem to think teens are nothing but a bunch of hoodlums, and so they're always scolding them and talking about "the good old days."

Synonyms: hooligan, riffraff, ruffian

hooligan

(*HOO-li-guhn*), noun

Someone else who is up to no good.

That kid who keeps getting detention must be a hooligan.

Synonyms: hoodlum, riffraff, ruffian

hotbed

(*HOT-bed*), noun

A place that encourages fast growth and spread of something, especially something unwanted.

The preschool classroom is a hotbed for germs—washing hands frequently is a must!

machinations

(*mak-uh-NEY-shuhnz*), noun

Dastardly, no-good schemes, plans, or plots.

The evil movie villain is a master of machinations, building crazy weapons to destroy the city.

miasma

(*mahy-AZ-muh*), noun

1. An eerie and dangerous mood.
2. Poisonous or smelly vapor.

There's a miasma in the horror movie right before the villain appears.

The Roots

Miasma comes from the Greek word *miainein*, which means "to pollute." So imagine a *miasma*-like smoke rising and spreading. The word hints that danger seeps into everything around it, just as pollution can.

mudslinging

(**MUHD**-sling-ing), noun

Lying about someone and trying to make people mistrust them.

I'm glad Alfred didn't resort to mudslinging in the Student Council election.

nemesis

(**NEM**-uh-sis), noun

Watch out! This is an opponent who will do anything to best you.

All superheroes must have a nemesis; otherwise,
they'd have no one to fight against!

Synonym: enemy

rabble-rouser

(**RAB**-uhl-rou-zer), noun

A person who is able to get a crowd overly excited or angry (generally to do something violent or for political reasons).

A lot of people thought Martin Luther King Jr. was
nothing but a rabble-rouser because his speeches always
made his listeners ready to fight for change.

rapscallion

(rap-**SKAL**-yuhn), noun

Someone who's up to no good.

Peter Pan was nothing but a rapscallion who didn't want to grow up!

Synonyms: hoodlum, hooligan, riffraff, ruffian, scallywag

riffraff

(**RIF**-raf), noun or adjective

1. *(noun)* A person or a group of people who are troublemakers.
2. *(adj.)* Worthless, trash.

Watch out for that gang of riffraff—they like to wait outside
the convenience store and swipe the candy you just bought!

Synonyms: hoodlum, hooligan, rapscallion, ruffian, scallywag

Level Up!

Some words in this book are reduplications—taking one word, then slightly altering it and slapping both together, like *knick-knack*, *hurly-burly* and *wishy-washy*. But *riffraff* is not a reduplication, although it seems like one. The term is taken from two Old French verbs—*rifler* (to spoil) and *raffler* (to carry off). Hmm, spoiling and stealing sure sound like things riffraff would do!

ruffian

(*RUHF-ee-uhn*), noun or adjective

1. *(noun)* A bully and rough person who is up to no good.
2. *(adj.)* Rough.

Evan was nothing but a ruffian who was always looking for ways to make fun of his cousin Lucy and push her around.

Synonyms: hoodlum, hooligan, rapscallion, riffraff, scallywag

scallywag (or scalawag)

(*SKAL-ee-wag*), noun

A person who's up to no good. (There are a lot of them in this book, huh?)

Pirates are generally nothing but a bunch of scallywags— they are always plotting how to steal more treasure!

Synonyms: hoodlum, hooligan, rapscallion, riffraff, ruffian

scofflaw

(*SKAWF-law*), noun

A person who repeatedly breaks rules or laws.

The school scofflaw never got detention, even though she was always in the hall without a hall pass!

snollygoster

(*SNOL-ee-gos-ter*), noun
A person who's clever in a bad, underhanded way.
In order to avoid getting into trouble, Richie was a snollygoster and planted false evidence in Sammy's locker.
Synonym: charlatan

toady

(*TOH-dee*), noun
A sidekick to a villain who is always complimenting them and doing whatever they say.
Mr. Smee is Captain Hook's toady—he is always right there to praise him and his villainous acts.
Synonym: lackey, yea-sayer, flunky

The Roots

The word *snollygoster* is thought to have come from playing with the name of the mythical creature known as the *snallygaster*. The beast was a combination of reptile and bird, with a sharp beak and claws. It originated from German immigrants in rural Maryland, near Washington, D.C. It is because of this proximity to our nation's capital that the term *snollygoster* is often used to mean a dishonest politician.

The Roots

Toady is thought to be a shortened form of "toad-eater," a person who was a charlatan's assistant. Charlatans traveled from town to town, selling bogus health remedies. The toad-eater would be planted in the audience to eat (or lick) a supposedly poisonous toad, and the onlookers would be fooled into thinking the toad-eater's miraculous survival was all due to the charlatan's medicine and potions.

usurp

(*yoo-**SURP***), verb

To take control without
permission or authority to do so.

*After watching those kid bakers
on TV, my sister decided to usurp
the kitchen from our mom and
make pies and cookies all day long.*

vendetta

(*ven-**DET**-uh*), noun

A feud or rivalry that goes
on for a long time.

*I think my dog has a vendetta with
the mailman—she has barked at
him daily since the day we got her!*

BLITZKRIEG
SKIRMISH

CATAPULT
PUGNACIOUS

FISTICUFF
BAZOOKA

FRACAS
DONNYBROOK

MUCKRAKER
QUIBBLE

PHALANX
BRANNIGAN

SQUABBLE
BRABBLE

OFF TO BATTLE

Words related to major clashes, feuds with foes, and all-out war

To launch an epic battle, you'll need epic words to describe all the action! Whether bombs unexpectedly rain down from a *catapult* on a battlefield, or you get surprised by a snowball fight walking home from school—you've just experienced a *blitzkrieg*! *Pugnacious* is a great new word to use for a soldier eager to fight, or that dog tugging on the leash to go after a cat. And in conflicts, people often let their fists fly in *fisticuffs*. But don't fight over these words, just use them!

bazooka

(*buh-ZOO-kuh*), noun

1. A rocket launcher used as a weapon by the military during a war.
2. A kazoo shaped like a trumpet.
3. A brand of bubblegum.

The bazooka won't be able to launch any missiles if there's a bunch of Bazooka gum stuck in it.

blitzkrieg

(*BLITS-kreeg*), noun

A lightning-fast, fierce attack, usually in a war or battle.

We launched a blitzkrieg of snowballs that started a huge snowball fight with the kids from the next block.

brabble

(*BRAB-uhl*), verb

To argue about something that isn't important.

Stop brabbling about whose dirty sock that is and please pick it up! (Said your mother to your brother.)

Pop Culture

Comedian Bob Burns entertained in the 1930s and '40s with a long trumpet-like kazoo he made from a pipe and called a bazooka (the Dutch word *bazuin* means "trumpet," and then Burns tacked the "ka" from "kazoo" on the end).

When the military invented the rocket launcher, it looked like Burns's instrument, so that's what they named it, a bazooka.

Then Bazooka bubble gum was introduced in 1947, shortly after the end of World War II. It was named after that rocket launcher used during the war. The gum was packaged in a patriotic red, white, and blue wrapper, included a small comic with every piece, and cost just a penny. Bazooka bubble gum creates big bubbles to pop, so its name is tied to the big bang of the Bazooka rocket launcher, not the kazoo hum of Burns's instrument.

brannigan

(*BRAN-i-guhn*), noun

A noisy fight.

The bossy brothers who butt heads got into a brannigan again and stopped talking to each other for an afternoon.

Synonym: donnybrook

catapult

(*KAT-uh-puhlt*), noun or verb

1. *(noun)* A large slingshot for launching objects, used as a weapon long ago.
2. *(verb)* To launch something.
3. *(verb)* To move suddenly.

As he approached the finish line, Alfred's feet suddenly sped up and catapulted him into first place!

Synonym: trebuchet, slingshot

The Roots

Both *catacombs* and *catapult* use the prefix *cata-*. But they don't mean close to the same thing! *Or do they?*

The Greek root *kata* means "down." *Catacombs* are underground, and a *catapult* hurls something up and away...which eventually must come down!

donnybrook

(*DON-ee-brook*), noun

A chaotic, wild, free-for-all fight.

All the hockey players in the donnybrook were ejected from the game because the referees couldn't tell who started the fight.

Synonym: brannigan

The Roots

The word *donnybrook* is named after a city near Dublin, Ireland. Beginning in the year 1204, Donnybrook, Ireland threw an annual fair. But in the mid-1800s, people threw a lot of punches during Donnybrook's festival! By 1855, the Donnybrook fair was forever canceled because of the wild fights that broke out there.

fisticuffs

(*FIS-ti-kuhf*), noun

A fight using the fists.

The verbal disagreement broke into fisticuffs when Alfred threw the first punch.

PUT 'EM UP!

fracas

(*FREY-kuhs*), noun

A noisy fight or uproar.

A fracas broke out between the cats in the alley, and it was so loud, it sounded like a bunch of wild tigers!

Synonyms: brannigan, donnybrook, ruckus, rumpus

muckraker

(*MUHK-reyk-r*), noun

Someone who exposes wrongdoing and corruption.

The middle school muckraker discovered the cafeteria wasn't recycling!

phalanx

(*FEY-langks*), noun

1.   A group of troops who fight closely together.
2.   A group of people who are working for a common goal or cause.

During a war, the phalanx can never relax when they are sneaking up on an enemy.

Synonyms: battalion, brigade

pugnacious

(*puhg-NEY-shuhs*), adjective

Eager to fight or argue.

That pug dog has a pugnacious attitude. He keeps growling at me.

quibble

(*KWIB-uhl*), noun or verb

1. *(noun)* A minor argument.
2. *(verb)* To bicker.

Don't quibble over the remote control—just give it to me!

skirmish

(*SKUR-mish*), noun

A minor argument or fight.

That troublemaker started another skirmish with his bothersome bragging.

squabble

(*SKWOB-uhl*), verb or noun

1. *(verb)* To argue about something you shouldn't even be arguing about.
2. *(noun)* The argument itself.

Don't squabble over the ice cream; you can both have another scoop!

trebuchet

(*TREB-yoo-shay*), noun

A large, medieval slingshot used for hurling rocks and bombs in warfare.

The trebuchet has a huge, spring-loaded arm that can hurl heavy things far away.

Synonym: catapult, slingshot

Pop Culture

The trebuchet is a medieval invention, but it has made a comeback in modern times for a specific purpose—tossing pumpkins! The sport is known as pumpkin chucking, or to make it rhyme and more fun to say, punkin chunkin. Contestants design and build a contraption to fling their pumpkin the farthest. Trebuchets, catapults, and slingshots are often the machine of choice, but sometimes cannons are used too.

MONSOON

TYPHOON ZEPHYR

CATACLYSM

SIROCCO TSUNAMI

FRIGORIFIC

HABOOB POGONIP

WUTHERING

FORCE OF NATURE

Words to describe wild and wicked weather

Sunny, windy, rainy, foggy—you're not going to find normal forecasts here! Depending on where you live, there are a lot of weather and climate conditions you may have never heard from your local meteorologist, like the dust storm called a *haboob*, or giant *tsunami* waves. If you live in the desert, you may have experienced a *sirocco*. And if it's sleeting, snowing, or ice storming, you know you're in for *frigorific* weather! Whether you're looking for new words to describe familiar conditions, or you're about to discover new ones, you'll soon be well prepared to weather what's ahead.

cataclysm

(**KAT**-uh-kliz-uhm), noun

1. A natural disaster related to an earthquake or flood.
2. Any disastrous situation.

When Mount Vesuvius erupted, the people of Pompeii barely had any warning to avoid the cataclysm of destruction the lava and ash caused.

frigorific

(*frig-uh-**RIF**-ik*), adjective

Causing or producing cold.

I have to put on thermal underwear because there's a frigorific wind blowing down from the Arctic!

haboob

(*huh-**BOOB***), noun

A dust storm or sandstorm.

If you ever decided to cross the Sahara Desert, be prepared for the haboob that can come out of nowhere—the wall of dust it brings makes it impossible to see anything.

monsoon

(*mon-**SOON***), noun

1. A stormy wind.
2. Rainy season, typically in southern Asia.

The monsoon led to flooding in the small town, damaging many of the roads and making it difficult for people to leave their homes.

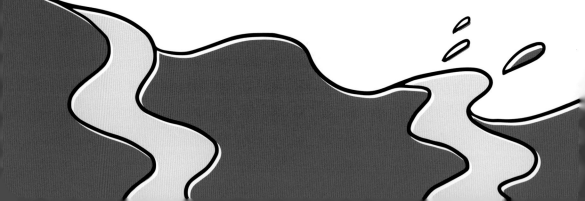

pogonip

(*POG-uh-nip*), noun

An ice fog.

While driving through the mountains, Alfred was amazed by the pogonip that seemed to come out of nowhere—not only could his dad no longer see clearly, but the windshield wipers suddenly had icicles on them!

sirocco

(*suh-ROK-oh*), noun

A hot and dusty wind.

The warm sirocco that blows off the Mojave Desert makes the air really heavy and dry.

Level Up!

Pogonip comes from the Shoshone Native Americans tribe, from a word *payinappih*, which means "cloud." A *pogonip* is an extremely rare phenomenon and needs specific weather conditions to form. The temperature must be below freezing, and the humidity (moisture) of the air must be near 100 percent to create the fog. If these two things happen simultaneously, ice crystals will form in the air. You are most likely to experience a *pogonip* in the mountain valleys in the American West, Alaska, or Siberia. Road trip, anyone?

tsunami

(*tsoo-**NAH**-mee*), noun

A giant wave like a wall of water.

After an earthquake, everyone who lives by the ocean needs to be prepared for the potential of a tsunami rising out of the water.

typhoon

(*tahy-**FOON***), noun

A violent storm like a hurricane that occurs in the eastern hemisphere.

A Category 1 typhoon is nothing but a really heavy thunderstorm. All it'll do is bring a lot of wind and rain. It's the Category 3 typhoon you gotta watch out for. It can wash away everything in its path.

wuthering

(***WUHTH**-er-ing*), adjective

Blowing hard and noisily.

Catherine cried out about her love for Heathcliff, but the wuthering wind meant that no one could hear her.

The Roots

A gentle breeze isn't wild, weird weather! It's calm. But its name is kind of wild, right?

Zephyr comes from the Greek *zephuros*, which means "god of the west wind." The ancient Greek believed there were gods for all four winds—north, south, east, and west—but the west wind was considered the gentlest, so its god was used to name a lightly blowing breeze.

zephyr

(*ZEF*-er), noun

Ahh, a light breeze.

Before going to bed, Penelope opened her window so the zephyr would keep her cool while she slept!

FLUMMERY

HANGRY

JUJUBE

GORGONZOLA

ESCARGOT

AMBROSIA

TIDBIT

FRANKENFOOD

CONCOCTION

UMAMI

INSIPID

GOBSTOPPER

BOUFFAGE

LOOFAH

NOM NOM NOM

Words for marvelous morsels and mealtimes

Food! Glorious food! We all need it; we all eat it! There are so many varieties of food that can be grown, cooked, baked, souped, and sandwiched. Feeling adventurous? Try some cooked snails, or *escargot*! Love to bake? Try your hand at a new *flummery*! There's a variety (or *smorgasbord*) of new words to let your taste buds give a try! (What do you have to lose? If you don't like them, you can always spit them out—but use a napkin, please.) You might want to have a snack handy while you read through this chapter, so you don't have a *borborygmus* (a grumbling tummy).

alfresco

(*al-**FRES**-koh*), adjective or adverb

To eat or do something out in the fresh air.

Alfred likes to dine alfresco on the patio with Penelope.

The Roots

The word *alfresco* is from the Italian *al fresco*, which means "in the fresh." While it is most generally used in relation to food and dining, *alfresco* can also describe a style of art that involves painting on top of fresh plaster. You'll find lots of alfresco restaurants *and* alfresco art if you visit Italy!

ambrosia

(*am-**BROH**-zhuh*), noun

1. The food of the Greek and Roman gods.
2. The most delicious thing you have ever tasted or smelled.
3. A type of dessert made with oranges and shredded coconut.

This chocolate-hazelnut spread is so out-of-this-world delicious—it's ambrosia!

Level Up!

In Greek mythology, *ambrosia* is the food of the gods and brings immortality to those who consume it. It can cure illness and erase years of wrinkles and other signs of old age. Its culinary partner is known as *nectar*, the drink of the gods.

borborygmus

(*bawr-buh-RIG-muhs*), noun

The sounds your tummy makes when you're hungry or gassy.

Those baked beans are making my tummy rumble with a loud borborygmus!

bouffage

(*boo-FAHJ*), noun

A satisfying meal.

After the bouffage of Alfred's favorite foods, he patted his stomach and burped!

croquembouche

(*kroh-kuhm-BOOSH*), noun

A pyramid of creampuffs held together with caramel that hardens to a crunch. In French, the word means "crack in the mouth."

Penelope is carefully stacking her creampuffs to make a croquembouche.

TEN WORDS THAT SOUND GROSS AND DISGUSTING BUT REALLY AREN'T

WORD	WHAT IT SOUNDS LIKE	WHAT IT REALLY MEANS
eggcorn	corn that tastes like eggs	confused idiom or saying
hogwash	a bath for a pig	nonsense
smellfungus	a smelly fungus	a cranky person who complains
mealymouth	a mouth full of a meal	not being honest and straightforward
egghead	a head shaped like an egg	book-smart, nerdy
logjam	a jam made from logs	a blockage
junket	a bunch of junk	a tour to promote something
lollygag	gagging on a lollipop	to waste time
logorrhea	a kind of diarrhea	a lot of talking
gumshoe	a shoe with gum stuck to it	a detective

concoction

(*kon-**KOK**-shuhn*), noun

A mixture of various things (usually with food and drink).

Penelope liked to try out new concoctions while baking—she once put dried grasshoppers in cookie dough to make chocolate chirp cookies!

escargot

(*es-kar-**GOH***), noun

Snails prepared as food. Yes, you can eat them!

He won't go to the restaurant that serves escargot because he thinks snails cooking will smell gross. (He should go. Escargot is delicious!)

fluffernutter

(***FLUHF**-uh-nuht-er*), noun

A cute, fluffy puppy!

Nah, sorry, it's really a sandwich made from marshmallow cream (brand name "Fluff") and peanut butter. (Although if you wanted to call a cute, fluffy puppy a fluffernutter, that would be adogable.)

I really love peanut butter and I really love s'mores, so when my mom made me a fluffernutter sandwich, I asked for a glass of chocolate milk to go with it!

flummery

(***FLUHM**-uh-ree*), noun

1. A bunch of sweet desserts.
2. A jelly or soft porridge.
3. Compliments or flattery that you don't really mean.

Penelope really loves to bake; she's always whipping up fresh batches of flummery for everyone to enjoy.

Frankenfood

(*FRANG*-kuhn-food), noun
A mash-up of Frankenstein + food. Food that has been changed or created through science.
Purple potatoes actually grow naturally and aren't Frankenfood.

Level Up!

The first Frankenfood was a tomato that had one of its genes duplicated in reverse so it wouldn't ripen as quickly. This tomato could stay on grocery shelves longer than ordinary tomatoes. Unfortunately, the variety of tomato they used wasn't very tasty, so the "Flavr Savr" tomato wasn't successful. It's no longer sold.

gobstopper

(*GOB*-stop-er), noun
A large piece of sucking candy.
Alfred could barely fit the gobstopper in his mouth—it was so huge, it looked like a baseball!
Synonym: jawbreaker

Pop Culture

In Roald Dahl's *Charlie and the Chocolate Factory*, candy-maker extraordinaire Willy Wonka invents the Everlasting Gobstopper. It will never get smaller, no matter how long a kid sucks on it.

gorgonzola

(*gawr-guhn-ZOH-luh*), noun
A smelly, moldy cheese that makes you hold your nose (but it actually tastes delicious)!
If you're picky about food, you'll groan at gorgonzola because of the smell, but you'll be missing out on a creamy, yummy cheese!

hangry

(*HANG-gree*), noun

Being mad and upset because you're starving. Hungry + angry.

Alfred gets hangry really quickly, so feed him fast before he starts yelling!

The Roots

Hangry is a really recent addition to the English language! It was added to the Merriam-Webster dictionary in September 2018. Lexicographers recorded its first use in a 1992 issue of *London Magazine*. From there it spread and became a part of everyday language—probably because it's a feeling everyone who's ever been super hungry can immediately understand.

hush puppy

(*HUHSH-puhp-ee*), noun

A ball of fried cornmeal dough, usually flavored with onion. Common in the southern U.S.; often served with seafood.

Hush puppies are the perfect finger food—they are the french fries of seafood.

insipid

(*in-SIP-id*), adjective

1. Bland and tasteless.
2. Not interesting, having no personality.

I don't get why people like seltzer so much; it's just insipid water with bubbles!

jujube

(*JOO-joob*), noun

A small Asian fruit that ripens to a wrinkled brown or purplish-black and looks like a date. When it's not ripe, it looks and tastes like an apple.

I wonder if people in Asia say, "To keep the doctor away, eat a jujube a day!"

kumquat

(*KUHM-kwot*), noun

A small, oval, yellow-orange Chinese citrus fruit.

At first I thought that kumquat was a tiny orange, but now that I've tasted it, I think it's the most delicious citrus fruit!

Pop Culture

When you go to the movies, peek inside the concession stand and you might see a green box of gummy candies called Jujubes. Jujubes have been around for over a hundred years, but don't look or taste like a real jujube fruit. The candy got its name from ju-ju gum, an ingredient that makes them stick-to-your-teeth chewy. Nowadays, Jujubes no longer have ju-ju gum in them, but they can still glue your teeth together (temporarily, of course)! Jujubes come in fruit flavors like lime, lemon, and cherry.

Level Up!

Kumquats are meant to be eaten skin and all. (Imagine if you had to peel something that tiny!) They are like an inside-out orange because the rind is the sweet part, not the fruit inside. The fruit has a sour flavor, so you should pop the whole thing in your mouth and enjoy the balance of sweet and sour.

loofah

(*LOO-fuh*), noun
An oblong vegetable, that when dried out, can be used as a bathing sponge.

It's weird to wash with a veggie, but a loofah makes really bubbly lather!

mawkish

(*MAW-kish*), adjective
1. Having a disgusting flavor that makes you want to barf.
2. Overly childish in the way you think and act.

Don't pour sour milk in your cereal unless you want it to be a mawkish breakfast!

muffuletta

(*muhf-uh-LET-uh*), noun
A sandwich from New Orleans made with a thick roll.

I'll take the muffuletta with mustard to go—because I don't want anyone seeing me trying to fit that huge roll in my mouth.

mulligatawny

(*muhl-i-guh-TAW-nee*), noun
A curry-flavored soup from India.

A bowl of mulligatawny is perfect on a cold winter day because it's so hot, spicy, and rich.

Level Up!

It's strange, but a loofah can either be eaten or made into a sponge! Before the vegetable ripens, it can be used for food. When it's fully ripened, it has too many chewy fibers to eat. Once it's dried out, all those intertwining fibers are what make it a good sponge. Don't keep your loofah sponge more than a month, though! It will go bad. (And then you definitely shouldn't eat it!)

The Roots

The word *mawkish* comes from disgusting roots. The Middle English word *mawke* means "maggot," the larva of a housefly that hatches on spoiled meat and other organic foods. Eww! But that's where the second definition comes in too—a maggot is an immature housefly!

persimmon
(*purr-SIH-mun*), noun
An orange-red Asian fruit that looks a little like a tomato.
A persimmon looks like a tomato, but you're supposed to eat it like an apple.

sassafras
(*SAS-uh-fras*), noun
A tree whose leaves and bark are used to flavor things that taste like root beer.
I love a sassafras soda with vanilla ice cream—it's a root beer float!

smorgasbord
(*SMAWR-guhs-bawrd*), noun
1. A buffet meal with every type of food you can imagine.
2. A bunch of different things collected in one place.
What a smorgasbord! I'll have some sausage, with potato salad, and macaroni and cheese, and snickerdoodles...

speculoos
(*SPEK-u-luhs*), noun
A cookie spiced with ginger, cinnamon, allspice, and cloves.
I can't decide if I want a snickerdoodle or speculoos for dessert, so I'll have both!

Level Up!

Speculoos is a traditional cookie baked in December for St. Nicholas Day in Holland, Belgium, and other European countries. It's like a shortbread cookie—made with sugar, butter, and flour. And like shortbread, speculoos cookies barely rise when baked.

succotash
(*SUHK-uh-tash*), noun
A dish of corn, beans, and peppers.
I would like succotash a lot more if it didn't have beans and peppers. Pass the corn, please.

sweetmeats
(*SWEET-meets*), noun
A sugary confection or candy.
It's a good thing sweetmeats are a dessert and not actually sweetened burger meat—that would be gross!

Pop Culture

The character Sylvester the Cat, who became popular on the *Looney Tunes* cartoons, is always trying to capture Tweety Bird for a delicious snack. But Tweety Bird is too smart for the bumbling housecat, and Sylvester is often left frustrated. His favorite phrase to utter whenever he's been tricked by Tweety is "Sufferin' succotash!" Sylvester says it with a lisp and a good amount of sputtering spit.

tidbit

(*TID-bit*), noun
1. A tiny but delicious bite of food.
2. A small piece of anything delightful.

We all want a tiny tidbit of every cake, cookie, and pie in the bakery!

umami

(oo-*MAH*-mee), noun
A meaty flavor. One of the basic tastes, along with sweet, sour, salty, and bitter.
When my dad grills burgers, the umami aroma makes my mouth water.

toadstool

(*TOHD*-stool), noun
A type of poisonous mushroom, often with a red-and-white spotted cap. Cute for drawing; bad for eating.
Robert loves finding wild mushrooms to cook for dinner, but he makes sure to stay away from toadstools—they looked cute, but made him really sick!

Pop Culture

The character Toad from the Super Mario video games wears a hat that looks like a toadstool. (Makes sense since he comes from the Mushroom Kingdom!)

toothsome

(*TOOTH*-suhm), adjective
Delicious and wonderful to eat.
These candies would be more toothsome if they didn't taste like medicine or stick to my teeth!

MEASURE UP!

Words for the big and small, fast and slow, straight and squiggly

Instead of using *big* or *small*, how about trying on these words for size: *infinitesimal* and *gargantuan*, or *flyspeck* and *peewee*. If you're a whiz at getting things done quickly, you should add *lickety-split* and *jiffy* to your vocabulary. And you might think being eighty years old makes you ancient, but it'd be pretty cool to call yourself an *octogenarian* one day. These words are guaranteed to be a lot of fun—or shall we say, *oodles* and *oodles* of fun. And there are even a few shapes thrown in for good measure. (Get it? Measure?)

abnormous

(*ab-**NAWR**-muhs*), adjective

Having an abnormal, irregular shape.

That is an enormous, abnormous fish. (Psst, it's a blobfish.)

apogee

(***AP**-uh-jee*), noun

1. The highest point or the peak.
2. The point in the moon's orbit when it is at its farthest point from the Earth. (The closest point is the perigee.)

Since it's the tallest mountain in the whole world, professional hikers consider climbing to the apogee of Mt. Everest to be the apogee of their career.

Synonym: pinnacle

beanpole

(***BEEN**-pohl*), noun

A very tall, skinny person.

The boy who blocked the basketball shot was a beanpole.

bulbous

(***BUHL**-buhs*), adjective

Shaped like a bulb, rounded and bulging.

Santa Claus has a bulbous belly (that jiggles like jelly).

bupkes

(***BUHP**-kiss*), noun

A whole lotta nothing! Nada, zero, zilch.

Everyone forgot my birthday and I got bupkes.

Synonyms: diddly-squat

caboodle

(*kuh-**BOOD**-l*), noun

A collection or bunch. Often used with "whole" ("the whole caboodle") or as part of the saying "kit and caboodle."

I double-checked my packing list for the trip, and I have everything I need—the camping kit and caboodle!

colossal

(*kuh-**LOS**-uhl*), adjective

Ginormous or ginormously powerful.

That's no ordinary monster—he's so colossal, he can rip a skyscraper off its foundation!

corkscrew

(*KORK-skroo*), adjective

A spiraling, looping, or zigzagging shape.

I can't wait to ride the corkscrew rollercoaster that zigs and zags in wild directions so fast!

The Roots

While the exact origin of *caboodle* is unknown, it most likely comes from the Dutch word *boedel*, which means "goods or property." The term *boodle* was also used to refer to a lot of something, often people or money. The expressions "kit and boodle" and "kit and caboodle" were both popular at the end of the 1800s, but the "caboodle" phrase stuck around—probably because of the fun alliteration. (Why it's spelled with a "c" instead of a "k" is anyone's guess!) It's very rare to find the word *caboodle* used on its own. However, there is also a brand of show caddies and cosmetic bags called Caboodles. (I'm guessing it was named so people can carry their whole kit and caboodle in their Caboodles!)

cornucopia

(*KOR-nuh-koh-pee-uh*), noun

1. A huge, never-ending supply of something (usually used with food or drink).
2. A container shaped like a goat's horn, used to hold flowers, fruit, and veggies.

After trick-or-treating, Alfred has a cornucopia of all his favorite candy—it'll probably take him till next Halloween to finish eating them all.

The Roots

In Greek mythology, the cornucopia is also known as the "horn of plenty." It was the horn of a goat that served as a nurse to baby Zeus, the god of all gods. This tale is so old that the exact origin of how the horn produced a bountiful supply of fruit and grains remains a mystery. But the horn of plenty was used as a symbol of the harvest by the Greeks, and now in America, it is used to symbolize the Thanksgiving holiday.

curlicue

(*KUR-lee-kyoo*), noun

A fancy, looping curl or twist.

Penelope has lovely penmanship and signs her name with curlicue Ps.

Pop Culture

Before the word *curlicue* arrived in the mid-1800s, we had the funny *curlie-wurlie!* In 1970, Cadbury Chocolate in the U.K. named a candy bar the "Curly Wurly" because it was shaped like a braid with intertwining chocolate ropes. In the U.S. it was named "Marathon" instead, and its wrapper had a ruler on it to show that it was long. However, it didn't stick around long and was discontinued in 1981.

diddly-squat

(*DID-lee-skwot*), noun

Nothing, nada, zilch, zero.

Alfred wants a candy bar, but he's got diddly-squat in his wallet to buy one.

Synonym: bubkes

dodecahedron

(*doh-dek-uh-HEE-druhn*), noun
A shape with twelve sides.
Alfred had to draw a dodecahedron for the geometry quiz but he drew an octagon, which was four sides short!

ephemeral

(*ih-FEM-er-uhl*), adjective
Lasting for a short amount of time.
Alfred thought the ephemeral white figure in the window was a ghost.

flyspeck

(*FLAHY-spek*), noun
A teeny-tiny little spot.
Earth is just a flyspeck in the vast universe.

gargantuan

(*gahr-GAN-choo-uhn*), adjective
Huge. Maybe even larger than ginormous.
King Kong is a gargantuan creature—he climbed the Empire State Building like it was a dollhouse.

Level Up!

Besides *dodecahedron*, there are names for shapes that you've probably never heard before, even though you might see those shapes every day. A doughnut's shape is called a *torus*. The capital letter "H" is a shape called a *balbis*. And the shape of the number 8 is a *lemniscate*, which translated from the Latin means "decorated with ribbons."

ginormous

(*jai-**NOR**-mus*), adjective
A portmanteau of *gigantic* and *enormous*. Bigger than both.
That wave was so ginormous I can't believe I rode it and no one saw me do it!

Level Up!

Some people think *ginormous* is a word that was recently created because it wasn't added to the Merriam-Webster dictionary until 2007. However, the first recorded use was way back in 1942, in a British newspaper. Military sailors coined *ginormous* as way to describe the extremely large things related to their work, like aircraft carrier ships, battles, or even the crowd in the British Navy cafeterias (known as the "mess hall").

humongous

(*hyoo-**MUHNG**-guhs*), noun
A possible mash-up of *huge* + *enormous* or *monstrous*. Bigger than both, but not as big as ginormous.
Alfred ate a humongous hoagie for lunch (and was too full to eat dessert).

infinitesimal

(*in-fin-i-**TES**-uh-muhl*), adjective
Extremely small or too teeny-tiny to measure.
An amoeba is so infinitesimal, you need a microscope to see it.

jiffy

(***JIF**-ee*), noun
A moment as quick as can be.
Finish showering in a jiffy and get dressed quickly so you're not late!

leviathan

(*luh-**VAHY**-uh-thuhn*), noun

1. Anything huge that has incredible power.
2. A sea monster.
3. A large sea animal, like a blue whale.

The Loch Ness Monster is a leviathan that lives in the waters of the Scottish Highlands. (Why didn't they just name it the Loch Ness Leviathan?)

lickety-split

(*LIK-i-tee-**SPLIT***), adverb

Really fast.

I finished licking my banana split lickety-split before it melted.

octogenarian

(*ok-tuh-juh-**NAIR**-ee-uhn*),

adjective or noun

Someone or something at least eighty years old (but less than ninety).

People are living longer and longer these days, generally well into their eighties—I can't wait to be an octogenarian!

oodles

(*OOD-lz*), noun

A whole lot of something.

Everyone loves oodles of buttered noodles piled high on their plate.

Level Up!

As far as anyone can tell, the word *oodles* entered the English language in 1869, but no one knows where it came from! Around the same time, pasta became popular in America. So maybe we can cook up an answer for ourselves.

Raw pasta is usually dried out, so when it's cooked, it soaks up the water and gets larger. Once it's done cooking, it looks like it's multiplied by magic! There's so much more than what you started with—you have "oodles of noodles"! This phrase is probably a reduplication, as we see with other fun words, and now *oodles* means a lot of something.

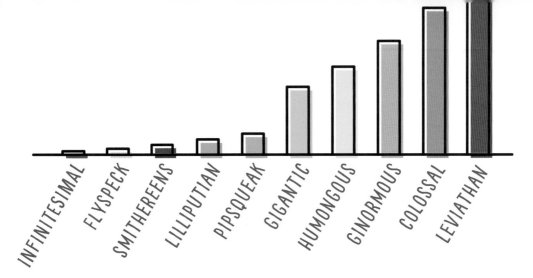

INFINITESIMAL · FLYSPECK · SMITHEREENS · LILLIPUTIAN · PIPSQUEAK · GIGANTIC · HUMONGOUS · GINORMOUS · COLOSSAL · LEVIATHAN

peewee
(*PEE-wee*), noun or adjective
1. *(noun)* Something tiny and unimportant.
2. *(adj.)* Tiny.
Don't call my little brother a peewee! He's only in first grade, and he's not done growing yet!

penultimate
(*peh-NUHL-tuh-mit*),
noun or adjective
The next to last.
In a ten-person race, ninth place is the penultimate prize.

picosecond
(*PEE-koh-sek-uhnd*), noun
One trillionth of a second.
It's impossible to go anywhere in a picosecond; it goes by too fast!

pip-squeak
(*PIP-skweek*), noun
Something or someone small and unimportant.
The cat chases the mouse around the house, but never catches the pip-squeak.

plethora
(*PLETH-er-uh*), noun
A lot of something, to the point that it's too much of something!
My little sister loves stuffed animals so much, she's got a plethora of plushies living on her bed and she sleeps on the floor instead.

smidgen

(*SMIJ-uhn*), noun

A tiny little bit.

My mom only lets me put a smidgen of whipped cream on my waffle, even though it's the best part!

smithereens

(*smith-uh-REENZ*), noun

Lots of teeny-tiny little bits and pieces.

Alfred dropped the glass and it smashed to smithereens.

sockdolager

(*sok-DOL-uh-jer*), noun

1. Something unusual or exceptional.
2. A knockout punch or something that settles a fight.

Each stone in an Egyptian pyramid is such a sockdolager that scientists still haven't figured out how they were lifted and moved to build it!

umpteen

(*UHMP-teen*), adjective

A large number, but you have no idea how large, because the exact amount doesn't matter—it's just a whole lot!

The girl asked her parents for a puppy on her birthday umpteen times, so she has no idea why she got a bicycle instead.

zenzizenzizenzic

(*zen-ZAHY-zen-ZAHY-zen-ZIK*), noun

An old mathematical term meaning to the eighth power, used before mathematicians invented the way to write it as x^8.

Can you imagine having to write zenzizenzizenzic every time you multiplied something to the eighth exponent?!

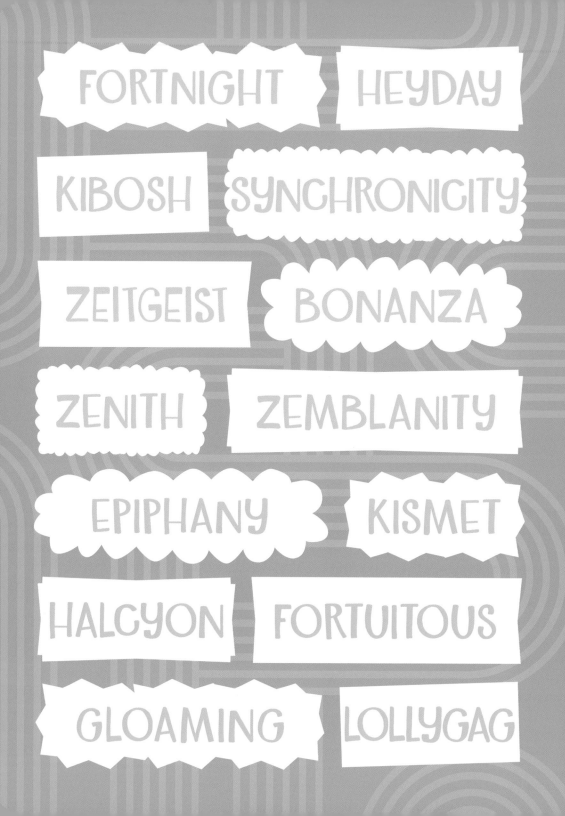

TIMING IS EVERYTHING

Words to describe special (and not-so-special) moments

You're in the middle of a great book or you've almost beat that video game level...and then you get called down for dinner—they just put the *kibosh* on your fun. Or maybe you've had an *epiphany*—an instant when you've figured out exactly how to get out of doing this week's chores or homework. Perhaps you found a $50 bill blowing around in the wind? That's quite a *bonanza*! Whether by chance, by nature, or by force, things generally happen at specific moments, and those moments need words to describe them. So here are a few to keep in your back pocket, so you can pull them out at just the right time.

bonanza

(*buh-**NAN**-zuh*), noun
An unexpected bunch of
good luck or good fortune.
*The baboon went bananas
over his banana bonanza.*

epiphany

(*ih-**PIF**-uh-nee*), noun
A sudden realization or
discovery of something
important or meaningful.
*Isaac Newton couldn't figure
out how gravity worked until an
apple fell from a tree and hit his
head—it gave him an epiphany!*
Synonym: discovery

fortnight

(*FAWRT-nahyt*), noun
Two weeks (fourteen days).
*Penelope thought her mom said
her loud cousin was only staying
"for the night," but she's really
staying a fortnight, which means
she'll have to share Penelope's
room for two whole weeks!*

Pop Culture

In 2017, the online game
Fortnite released and
immediately became one
of the most popular video
games in the world, with
over 100 million players.
The title of the game is
based on fort-building,
though, which is how
your player survives mon-
ster and zombie attacks.
There's a "Save the World"
mode that lasts for a
two-week time period, so
the real word's meaning
is still in there. (And kids
might love it so much that
they play Fortnite for two
weeks straight!)

fortuitous

(*for-TOO-i-tuhs*), adjective

Lucky or having good fortune.

It was fortuitous that I moved next door to you—because you taught me how to make videos, and now I've got my own channel!

gloaming

(*GLOH-ming*), noun

Twilight or dusk, after the sun has gone down but it is still light outside. The sky remains a dark blue and seems to color everything with a blue tint.

I like to take a walk in the gloaming and watch the sky darken.

halcyon

(*HAL-see-uhn*), adjective

A time in the past when great things happened.

Old people always seem to miss the halcyon days of their youth—I just miss those halcyon days of preschool: naps, snacks, and no homework!

heyday

(*HAY-day*), noun

A time of extraordinary success.

The cheer team's heyday was two years ago, when we won the State Championship and traveled to Florida for Nationals.

kibosh

(*KAHY-bosh*), noun
Something that puts a
stop to something.
*The kid put the kibosh on the
kickball game—he kicked the
ball so hard that it deflated.*
Synonym: end, conclusion, halt

Level Up!

As the word *caboodle* is only
used in the phrase "kit and
caboodle," and never on its
own, *kibosh* only tends to
be heard in the common
phrase "put the kibosh on,"
which means to put a stop
to something, either on
purpose or by accident.

kismet

(*KIZ-mit*), noun
Something that is
totally meant to be.
*It was kismet that Alfred
and Penelope met.*
Synonyms: serendipity,
fate, destiny

lollygag

(*LOL-ee-gag*), verb
To waste time and fool around.
*Stop lollygagging around the
candy store and staring at the
lollipops. Just buy one already!*

overmorrow

(*oh-ver-MAWR-oh*), noun
The day after tomorrow.
*My birthday is overmorrow,
so you only have today and
tomorrow to get me a gift!*

synchronicity

(*sing-kruh-NIS-i-tee*), noun
When actions or thoughts
happen at the same time,
without explanation. Can
also be when a prediction or
dream comes true by chance.
*Penelope texted Alfred right
as he was calling here—talk
about synchronicity!*
Synonym: synergy

zeitgeist

(*TSAHYT-gahyst*), noun

The mood, feeling, and culture of a certain time in history.

The zeitgeist during the founding of America was one of hope, pride, and independence.

zemblanity

(*zem-**BLAN**-uh-tee*), noun

The act of making unhappy, expected discoveries—the complete opposite of serendipity.

As zemblanity would have it, Mom's unsalted mashed potatoes were bland and blech.

zenith

(*ZEE-nith*), noun

1. The most successful time— the highest point or peak.
2. The part of the sky that's right over your head.

Penelope thinks that winning an Oscar, or at least a Kids' Choice Award, would be the zenith of her acting career!

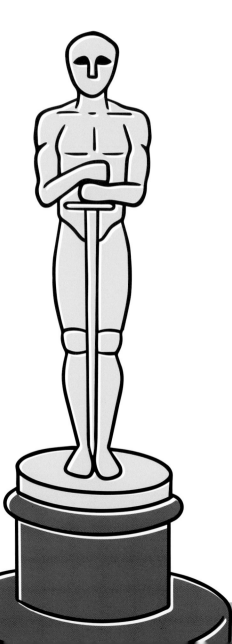

SCUTTLEBUTT NOODGE

GASBAG RIGAMAROLE

BLOVIATE CLAPTRAP

PIFFLE BOMBINATE

HARRUMPH BABBLE

OROTUND GIBBERISH

CATERWAUL BLUBBER

MOTOR-MOUTH

Words for loud people and those who love to chitchat

Your sister seems to never stop talking (she's so *loquacious*). You have that friend who can never keep a secret (what a *bigmouth*). You never have a clue what that one teacher is talking about (they seem to speak only in *gibberish*). You're hoping you're never the source of gossip (*clishmaclaver*) in the school hallways. Enough of this rambling *yakety-yak*! Let these words speak for themselves!

babble

(*BAB-uhl*), verb or noun

1. *(verb)* To produce speech or words that can't be understood.
2. *(noun)* Meaningless noise or foolish talk.

My baby sister babbles nonstop; too bad none of us can understand whatever she's trying to say!

Synonyms: bafflegab, gibberish, gobbledygook, jabberwocky; jibber, jabber, prattle

The Roots

"The Tower of Babel" is a Biblical story that offers an explanation about why there are many different languages in the world. In the story, when people still spoke one common language, they decided to build a high tower to reach God. But they did this to make a name for themselves, not to serve God. So, God punished the people by confusing their speech so they could not understand each other, then he scattered them around the world.

bafflegab

(*BAF-uhl-gab*), noun

A bunch of words that can't be understood.

The instructions on this game are so complicated, they read like bafflegab.

Synonyms: gibberish, gobbledygook, jabberwocky

bigmouth

(*BIG-mouth*), noun

A loud, noisy person who says things they shouldn't.

Too bad the bigmouth at the game wasn't a cheerleader too— because everyone heard him!

Synonyms: blabbermouth

blabbermouth

(*BLAB-er-mouth*), noun

Someone who talks a lot and says things they shouldn't.

Stop telling everyone my secret, you blabbermouth!

Synonyms: bigmouth

blatherskite

(*BLATH-er-skahyt*), noun

1. A person who talks a lot of nonsense.
2. Nonsense talk.

Don't listen to Alfred's blatherskite about how to do halfpipe tricks; he can barely snowboard and has no idea what he's talking about.

bloviate

(*BLOH-vee-eyt*), verb

When someone talks a lot about how great they are (but they really aren't all that great). They pump themselves up to look better.

If he doesn't stop bloviating about all his video game high scores, I'm going to go home.

blubber

(*BLUHB-er*), verb

To cry and try to speak at the same time, noisily and snottily. (Use a tissue, not your sleeve!)

The toddler blubbered over his balloon, crying and calling after it as it floated away.

bombinate

(*BOM-buh-neyt*), verb

To make a buzzing or humming sound.

Stay away from that tree because I see a beehive— and now I hear it bombinating!

caterwaul

(*KAT-er-wawl*), verb

1. To howl or cry in long, drawn-out wails.
2. To fight like cats.

The loud sound in the alley was stray cats caterwauling as they competed over the scraps in the trash.

chatterbox

(**CHAT**-er-boks), noun

A person who talks nonstop.

You can't just chitchat with a chatterbox because they will go on and on.

Synonym: blabbermouth

claptrap

(**KLAP**-trap), noun

Nonsense.

I don't like to talk about claptrap, so stop telling me lies!

Synonym: clishmaclaver

clishmaclaver

(**KLISH**-muh-klay-ver), noun

Gossip.

Repeating clishmaclaver isn't nice behavior, but sometimes it's just so juicy, I can't resist a good rumor!

Synonym: claptrap

confabulation

(*kuhn-fab-yuh-**LEY**-shuhn*), noun

Conversation and discussion. (And it could be fabulous, but doesn't have to be.)

The debate team had a confabulation about their take on detention—they shared arguments about how to get rid of it!

gasbag

(**GAS**-bag), noun

Someone who talks about how wonderful they are...all the time.

That gasbag reminds us every day how smart and handsome he is—but he's full of hot air!

Synonyms: windbag

gibberish

(*JIB-er-ish*), noun

Speech or writing that makes no sense, usually with complicated words that few people understand.

The professor used so many long and complicated words in the sentence that it sounded like gibberish!

Synonym: gobbledygook, jabberwocky

gobbledygook

(*GOB-uhl-dee-gook*), noun

A bunch of words that make no sense.

I couldn't understand Alfred's gobbledygook when he tried to speak with his mouth full of gummy worms.

Synonyms: babble, bafflegab, gibberish, jabberwocky

grandiloquent

(*gran-DIL-uh-kwint*), adjective

Meant to be grand, but sounding ridiculous instead.

My little sister is so cute when she makes a grandiloquent speech to our parents about being old enough to stay up late.

Synonyms: bombastic, highfalutin, pompous

guttural

(*GUHT-er-uhl*), adjective

Making a deep, harsh sound that comes from the back of the throat.

I know I'm in trouble when my dad yells my full name with a guttural rattle in his throat!

harrumph

(*HUH-ruhmf*), verb

A sound you make when you're upset or disappointed.

Penelope harrumphed and put her hands on his hips—she wasn't happy.

jibber-jabber
(*JIB-er-JAB-er*), verb
To talk a lot of gibberish (nonsense).
Babies are so cute—I love how they jibber-jabber away
like we have any clue what they are saying!

logorrhea
(*law-guh-REE-uh*), noun
Talk that spews and spills and keeps coming and coming and doesn't
stop and doesn't make a lot of sense. (Diarrhea of the mouth. Eww.)
People think Lola is shy, but once you get her talking,
it's like she has logorrhea—she won't stop!

loquacious
(*loh-KWAY-shuhs*), adjective
Running your mouth all the time; extremely talkative.
Anne of Green Gables was known for being quite
loquacious—she spent the whole drive talking Matthew's
ear off! (But thankfully, he didn't mind.)

motormouth
(*MOH-ter-mouth*), noun
Someone who talks nonstop, like they are being powered by a motor!
That motormouth talks so much, I can never get a word in myself!

mumbo jumbo
(*MUHM-boh JUHM-boh*), noun
A bunch of words that sound like absolute nonsense
and therefore cause a lot of confusion.
The magician distracted the audience by mumbling a
bunch of mumbo jumbo, like "abracadabra" and "hocus-
pocus," while he made his assistant disappear.

murmuration

(*mur-muh-REY-shuhn*), noun

1. The act of murmuring (making a low humming noise or mumbling).
2. A flock of birds called starlings that fly closely together in large groups, swerving and swooping quickly. They appear to move as one.

Penelope began a steady stream of murmuration to calm herself down as she walked through the park—humming took her mind off the murmuration of black birds swooping from tree to tree.

noodge

(*nooj*), verb or noun

1. *(verb)* To nag and complain in a whiny, annoying way.
2. *(noun)* Someone who's an annoying pest.

Stop noodging her—she won't tell you about the surprise party on Friday!

orotund

(*OAR-uh-tuhnd*), adjective

1. Having a strong, booming voice.
2. Overblown and exaggerated in manner of speaking.

Everyone in the stands can hear the coach on the football field because he's got such an orotund voice.

piffle

(*PIF-uhl*), noun or verb

1. *(noun)* Nonsense talk.
2. *(verb)* To talk nonsense.

His piffle is like a riddle, I can't figure out what he's saying!

raconteur

(*rak-uhn-**TUR***), noun

Someone who tells an interesting, fascinating story that
you'd want to listen to all day. The best storyteller.

*As the raconteur recounted his adventure in the rain forest, more
people stepped forward to listen because his tale was so fantastic.*

rigamarole

(***RIG***-*uh-muh-rohl*), noun

1. Confusing and meaningless conversation.
2. A complicated and time-consuming process
   that doesn't need to be so complicated.

Why wrestle with the rigamarole of tying your shoes when there's Velcro?

schmooze

(*shmooz*), verb

To chitchat and socialize with someone in a way that
makes them like you. You may schmooze to gain
favor with someone or to get something.

*Alfred schmoozes with the girls at the dance
so they'll invite him to their parties.*

Synonym: hobnob

scuttlebutt

(***SKUHT***-*l-buht*), noun

A rumor—information that spreads around,
but no one knows if it's true or not.

*Penelope wanted to know who started the scuttlebutt about her
having a crush on Alfred that was going around the neighborhood.*

windbag

(*WIND-bag*), noun

Someone who talks a lot but says nothing worthwhile—their chatter is exhausting.

That windbag sure likes to talk about all the awards he almost won—he can go on for hours and hours and hours, even though no one cares!

Synonyms: gasbag

yackety-yak

(*YAK-i-tee-YAK*), noun or verb

Nonstop, loud, and unimportant chitchat.

Alfred and his friends yackety-yak on the phone all the time instead of messaging and texting like everyone else.

yammer

(*YAM-er*), noun or verb

1. *(noun)* Loud, nonstop talking.
2. *(verb)* To complain...and whine...and complain again.

When my aunt comes over, she and my mom yammer in the kitchen all day so that even the neighbors can hear them.

Pop Culture

In 1958, a rock 'n' roll band named the Coasters released a song called "Yakety Yak." It's about parents telling a teenager to do his chores or he can't go out with his friends on Friday night. The teen isn't too happy, and says "yackety-yak" as a way to complain about their nonstop demands (and probably 'cause he doesn't think doing his chores is as important as hanging with his friends). But in the song, his parents respond with a clear warning, "Don't talk back!"

BALDERDASH GUFFAW

DROLL COCKAMAMIE

LAMPOON LUDICROUS

MIRTH FIDDLE-FADDLE

POPPYCOCK TITTER

CHORTLE WISECRACK

TOMMYROT STOOGE

CLASS CLOWN

Words about silliness, belly laughs, and being a comedian

You tell a great joke, and everyone is laughing—they're *guffawing*, *chortling*, and *tittering*! If you're known as the class clown, or hope to be a comedian someday, let's get you more words to help you set the stage for *wisecracks* and *waggery*. You know that everyone loves a good laugh, but as long as you're not laughing at people's mistakes—that's called a *schadenfreude*, by the way— feel free to *jest* and *josh* away!

afterwit

(*AF-ter-wit*), noun

A hilarious, witty, perfect comeback...
that you think of when it's too late.

*When someone pokes fun at Alfred, he doesn't have a clever
comeback until he thinks of an* afterwit *the next day.*

balderdash

(*BAWL-der-dash*), noun or interjection

Exaggerated nonsense.

You can't eat a six-layer chocolate cake in sixty seconds! Balderdash!

Synonyms: bunkum, fiddle-faddle, hogwash,
hokum, hooey, horsefeathers, poppycock

boffola

(*BOF-oh-lah*), noun

A good, loud belly laugh.

Santa may be jolly, but he can't make a boffola *while
delivering gifts or he'll wake up the kids!*

bunkum

(*BUHNG-kuhm*), noun

Complete nonsense that is purposefully phony or false.

Billy was talking bumkum *when he bragged about
the ghost that lives in his basement.*

Synonyms: fiddle-faddle, hogwash, hokum, hooey

chortle

(*CHOR-tul*), verb

Laughing quietly or to yourself when amused or pleased.

*Penelope didn't want to laugh at Alfred's joke, but
she couldn't help letting out a little* chortle.

cockamamie

(*KOK-uh-mey-mee*), adjective
Something incredibly ridiculous.

A chocolate river, wallpaper you can lick, soda that can make you fly—what a bunch of cockamamie inventions! There's no way those are real!

crow

(*kroh*), verb
A really loud black bird. Gotcha! In this context, it means to laugh in a loud, shrill way—sounding very much *like* the bird!

My grandpa doesn't just laugh—he begins to crow, which echoes through the whole house!

droll

(*drohl*), adjective or noun
1. *(adj.)* Amusing, odd, or funny.
2. *(noun)* A person or thing that is funny or has funny characteristics.

In the fairy tale, Rumpelstiltskin is a droll little man—especially his name, it's so oddly funny.

Level Up!

A *cockamanie* was known as a temporary tattoo, a fad that made its way to the U.S. through Europe in the early 1900s. The original French word, *decalcomanie* (you'll notice the word *decal* in there), was often mispronounced by Americans, who dropped the first syllable and would say *calcomanie*. Passed around by children, many of whom were immigrants who spoke more than one language, the word morphed into *cockamamie*. Then, because the tattoos were so inexpensive and, well, *temporary*, the word began being used for things that had little lasting value. This was further twisted into meaning the silly, absurd, or ridiculous. It may sound *cockamamie*, but it's true!

fiddledeedee

(*fid-l-dee-DEE*), interjection
An expression you use when
someone else is talking
nonsense and you want to
dismiss what they say.
*Fiddledeedee! There's no way
you can beat me in a run!*
Synonyms: balderdash, bunkum,
fiddle-faddle, hogwash, hokum,
hooey, horsefeathers, poppycock

fiddle-faddle

(*FID-l-fad-l*), noun or interjection
Nonsense. Can also be used as
an interjection like *fiddledeedee*.
*Oh, fiddle-faddle, how am I
supposed to row this boat when
it doesn't even have a paddle?!*
Synonyms: balderdash, bunkum,
fiddledeedee, hogwash, hokum,
hooey, horsefeathers, poppycock

Pop Culture

Fiddle-faddle comes from
the word *fiddlesticks* by
doubling or playing with
the word "fiddle." *Fiddle-
faddle* is also the name of a
candy-coated popcorn with
peanuts, similar to Cracker
Jack, but there's no prize
inside. Oh, *fiddlesticks!*

fiddlesticks

(*FID-l-stiks*), interjection
Something you say when
you're annoyed.
*Fiddlesticks! My shoes got
stuck in the mud again!*
Synonyms: egads, gadzooks

guffaw

(*guh-FAW*), noun or verb
Bwaaaaaaa-haaaa! Loud
laughter! Sounds like it
comes from the gut!
*My grandpa doesn't just
laugh—he makes a guffaw that
you can hear across the street!*

hogwash

(*HAWG-wosh*), noun

Nonsense and baloney.

You're going to give a hog a wash? That's hogwash!

Synonyms: balderdash, bunkum, fiddle-faddle, hogwash, hokum, hooey, horsefeathers, poppycock, tommyrot

The Roots

If you think *hogwash* comes from a pig bath, you'd be wrong. The *wash* part of the word actually meant leftover food scraps. *Hogwash* was literally food for swine. This kitchen waste was otherwise useless—plus very few of us own pigs these days—so *hogwash* evolved to mean "worthless." If something is worthless, it's not worth your time or thought, and therefore "nonsense"—just like washing a pig would be! (They'd only roll out of the bath and get right back into the mud!)

hokum

(*HOH-kuhm*), noun

1. Lines in a play, performance, or speech that exist only for the laughs.
2. Pretentious nonsense of any kind.

People who are competitive love to talk trash, but most of it is nothing but hokum.

Synonyms: bunkum, fiddle-faddle, hogwash, hooey

horsefeathers

(*HORS-feh-therz*), interjection

Complete and utter nonsense.

Horsefeathers! Horses don't have feathers!

Synonyms: balderdash, bunkum, fiddle-faddle, fiddledeedee, hogwash, hokum, hooey, poppycock, tommyrot

lampoon

(*lam-POON*), verb or noun

1. *(verb)* To ridicule and make fun of someone or something.
2. *(noun)* Public criticism, using sarcasm, irony, or humor.

Memes can be really funny and are meant to generate laughs, but they aren't as much fun if you're the one being lampooned.

laughingstock

(**LAF**-ing-stok), noun

A person or thing that is the butt of a joke.

Alfred didn't realize that Toby had taped a "Kick Me" sign on to his back, making him a laughingstock as he walked down the hallway.

ludicrous

(loo-**DA**-kris), adjective

So weird, over-the-top, or ridiculous that it makes you laugh.

Penelope thought Alfred looked absolutely ludicrous dressed as a taco for Halloween!

Synonym: comical

mirth

(*murth*), noun

Joy or laughter.

Watching puppies explore their surroundings is sure to bring mirth to anyone with a heart!

nincompoop

(**NIN**-kuhm-poop), noun

Someone who's foolish.

Alfred is an even bigger nincompoop for trying to roller skate with an ice cream cone with five scoops—he barely knows how to skate!

poppycock

(**POP**-ee-kok), adjective or noun or interjection

Absolute nonsense!

Poppycock! You are can't be related to both the Queen of England and the President of the United States!

Synonyms: balderdash, bunkum, fiddle-faddle, fiddledeedee, hogwash, hokum, hooey, horsefeathers

schadenfreude

(*SHAHD-n-froi-duh*), noun
Happiness about someone's
mistakes or misfortunes.
*The skateboarding show-
off missed his halfpipe stunt
and the other competitors
felt schadenfreude.*

slapstick

(*SLAP-stik*), adjective or noun
A kind of humor that
features a lot of pratfalls,
exaggerated funny faces,
and silly, rowdy action.
*The clown slapped a pie in
the ringmaster's face during
his slapstick routine.*

snigger

(*SNIH-gur*), verb
To laugh, but try and cover it up.
*The whole class couldn't help
but snigger when they found out
that Penelope and Alfred would
have to kiss in the school's play.*
Synonym: snicker, titter

Pop Culture

A slapstick comedy fea-
tures rough-and-tumble
play—funny falls, jabs, and
pokes. It gets the name
from an actual slapstick—
which was two sticks fas-
tened together to make a
loud slapping noise. Come-
dians and clowns used it to
pretend to slap someone
across the face (because
it wouldn't be cool to *actually* slap someone, even if
you're just joking around!).
The Three Stooges, a
comedy trio, were masters
of slapstick comedy and
also used weird *boing*-ing
sound effects to highlight
their wild wallops.

stooge

(*stooj*), noun or verb

1. (*noun*) A character who plays second fiddle to the main character and is often the butt of all the jokes.
2. (*verb*) To act like someone's puppet, sidekick, or subordinate.

Alfred tried out for the lead in the play, but got cast as a minor character used for comic relief—he wasn't happy about being the stooge.

titter

(*TIT-er*), verb

To laugh in a covered-up or nervous way.

When their new teacher said his name was Mr. Wacko, the class couldn't help but titter—they knew they shouldn't laugh, but it sounded so funny!

Synonym: snicker, snigger

tomfoolery

(*tom-FOO-luh-ree*), noun

Any kind of silliness.

Babies are easily entertained by tomfoolery—making funny faces and noises always gets them giggling.

Synonyms: baboonery

Pop Culture

The Three Stooges were a group of three men who performed comedy acts on stage and in film for fifty years. Their work was filled with slapstick humor that included pratfalls, eye-poking, head-bonking, and other silly antics. Between 1934 and 1946, they starred in about a hundred and ninety short comedy films and became world famous. Their films were generally only twenty minutes long, and you can still catch them through TV reruns or online. While the three guys in the Three Stooges switched and swapped over the years, the original "wise guys"—Larry, Curly, and Moe—are the trio that fans remember most.

tommyrot

(*TOM-ee-rot*), noun

Nonsense and foolishness.

Tommy tries to avoid any sort of tommyrot, so that no one would get the silly idea that the word was named after him.

waggery

(*WAH-gur-ree*), noun

1. Joking around! Playing practical jokes.
2. Mischievous laughter.

Alfred gets up to all kinds of waggery on April Fool's Day! Thankfully his mischief makes everyone laugh.

wisecrack

(*WAHYZ-krak*), noun or verb

1. (*noun*) A snarky, sarcastic joke or pun.
2. (*verb*) To say something in a snarky or sarcastic way.

Bobby, the class clown, always gets in trouble for his wisecracks.

wisenheimer

(*WAHY-zuhn-hahy-mer*), noun

Someone who makes a lot of snarky jokes.

Bobby learned all of his best jokes from his brother, Alfred, who is a natural wisenheimer.

APPARATUS GADGET

QUEUE BUMBLEDOM

SPITTOON SQUEEGEE

MOJO NICKELODEON

LOOPHOLE ZARF

PAPYRUS TALISMAN

DUMBWAITER ELIXIR

COMES IN HANDY

Words for useful things (and a few that are no help at all)

You need something done, and we've got the right word—and the right tool—for you. From the simple *bumbershoot* that keeps you dry in a rainstorm, to a complicated *apparatus* with multiple gears and levers, these things will get the job done. Even if you don't remember what the tool is called, simply grab that *gizmo* and get to work! But beware, some of these things could create a *logjam* and make a job more difficult, so learn these words and help yourself out.

apparatus

(*ap-uh-**RAT**-uhs*), noun
A complicated machine, instrument, or tool for a specific purpose.
My mousetrap apparatus has tons of levers, springs, and cheese, but no mouse!
Synonym: device

bumbershoot

(*BUHM-ber-shoot*), noun
An umbrella—a mash-up made from umbrella + parachute.
Shoot, it's raining and I don't have a bumbershoot!

bumbledom

(*BUHM-buhl-duhm*), noun
The behavior and work that a proud and cocky government employee does—except they actually aren't very good at their job!
Alfred thinks he's so important because his classroom job is official pencil sharpener—but we all know it's nothing but bumbledom.

Pop Culture

Bumbershoot is the name of an annual arts and music festival in Seattle, probably because the city is known for its frequent rainy weather. The word *bumbershoot* appeared in a song from the classic children's film *Chitty Chitty Bang Bang*. In the tune, bumbershoot is sung to near-rhyme with "bamboo" as the performers dance with bamboo sticks. The movie is set in England, and many characters speak with British accents, leading people to mistakenly believe bumbershoot is of English origin. Nope, it's very much American, and so fun to say that we "oot" to use it more, especially on a rainy day!

dumbwaiter

(*DUHM-wey-ter*), noun
A waiter who brings you the wrong order. (Kidding!) It's a small elevator in an apartment building, house or restaurant to easily move things like food or garbage up and down floors.
Installing a dumbwaiter in a hundred-story house is a smart idea; it'd make it easier to move things from floor to floor!

elixir

(*ih-LIK-ser*), noun
A potion used to cure an illness or to grant magical qualities. (Today it is often used to mean *anything* that can fix whatever's wrong—physical, mental, social—you name it!)
People are always on a quest to find the Elixir of Life so that they will never grow old and have immortality!

flotsam

(*FLOT-suhm*), noun
Junk found floating on a body of water, but it can also mean any useless little thing.
The ducks fluttered around the pond all week, and when they finally flew away, they left behind feathery flotsam.

Pop Culture

"Flotsam and jetsam" is a common saying in sea travel and means items that once belonged to a ship. All "flotsam" floats, and "jetsam" is something jettisoned—or tossed—off a ship to make the load lighter. There is actually a third word that was lost from this phrase, *lagan*, which means things thrown from a ship with a buoy so they float and can be found again. But you may also know Flotsam and Jetsam as the sea-witch Ursula's two nasty moray eel minions in the animated Disney feature *The Little Mermaid*.

gadget

(*GAJ-it*), noun

A cool tool.

My brother bought this gadget for coding secret messages by using numbers—you spin it around and each number matches a different letter.

Synonyms: gizmo, widget

gizmo

(*GIZ-moh*), noun

1. Something that does something really cool.
2. A gadget that has a name but you don't know it or can't remember it.

At the Fourth of July fireworks show, our town has these gizmos staked into the ground that spin, whistle and shoot sparks!

Synonyms: gadget, widget

Pop Culture

Back in the 1940s, there were a bunch of slang words that all began with g and all meant the same thing: a gadget whose name you can't recall, or isn't important enough to know in the first place. *Gizmo*, though, has hung around longer than *gazinkus*, *gazunkus*, *gigamaree*, and *gingambob*.

haberdasher

(*HAB-er-dash-er*), noun

A store or person who sells clothing and accessories for men.

The haberdasher offers handsome top hats, suits, and ties.

jetsam

(*JET-suhm*), noun

Things on a boat thrown into the water on purpose, to lighten the load. Unlike flotsam, jetsam doesn't float.

When the crew realized the boat was too heavy and sinking, they began tossing stuff into the ocean—anything with no value became jetsam.

logjam

(*LAWG*-jam), noun or verb
1. (*noun*) A blockage or pileup of things.
2. (*verb*) To block so that nothing can get through.

The lunch line was logjammed, and Alfred was worried he wouldn't be able to get any jam before the bell rang.

The Roots

The word *logjam* comes from an actual jam of logs! When loggers cut down trees, there is often a waterway to carry the logs away from the site. The heavy logs float, so they are easy to transport this way—as long as the waterway doesn't clog with too many logs! When it does, it's a logjam. (*Log-clog* would be a good word for it too.)

loophole

(*LOOP*-hohl), noun
Something that lets you escape from a rule or responsibility.
Penelope was hoping to find a loophole to get out of doing her chores for the week.

mojo

(*MOH-joh*), noun
A kind of magical power that cannot be explained.
Alfred rubbed his lucky rabbit's foot to get some mojo for the swim meet.

moniker

(*MON-i-ker*), noun
A nickname for "nickname."
Alfred doesn't like the moniker "Al" and won't answer if you call him that.

moolah

(*MOO-law*), noun

Slang for money—usually when you mean A LOT of money.

Penelope got a lot of moolah for her birthday, and she put almost all of it in the bank.

nickelodeon

(*nik-uh-LOH-dee-uhn*), noun

1. An old-time theater where movies or live shows could be watched. The ticket cost a nickel.
2. A jukebox (old-fashioned music player) that costs a nickel to use.

Man, I can't believe people could just pay five cents to see a movie! Why aren't there any nickelodeons today?!

Level Up!

There are many slang words for money. In America, there's *bacon*, *bread*, *cabbage*, *cheddar*, *dough*, and *kale*, to name a few.

Did you notice what those words have in common? They're all types of food! Why? It could be because food is necessary to live, and so is money, but no one has been able to prove that link for sure. The first food word used to mean money was *dough*, in the mid-1800s. (It makes sense, then, that bread came later...because dough gets baked into bread.)

Pop Culture

The word *nickelodeon* is a mash-up of the word *nickel* (as in the coin) and the word *melodeon*, which meant "music hall." *Melodeon* has two potential origins—either from *melodie*, the French word for "melody" or the Greek word *oideion* (building for musical performances). In the mid-1800s, when nickelodeons got their start in the U.S., they offered entertainment of all kinds.

However, in 1979, *Nickelodeon* took on a new meaning when it became the name for the first twenty-four-hour cable TV channel that was just for kids. Its creator said he named the channel Nickelodeon because its shows were entertaining like the theaters, plus "the sound of the word was nice and rolled off the tongue easily." From 1986 to 1994, one of Nickelodeon's most popular programs was *Double Dare*, a game show where kids answered trivia questions and performed crazy physical challenges. Many challenges include sliding in or around green slime. (It seems the concept was pretty popular, 'cause *Double Dare* had a revival in 2000 and 2018!)

Green slime appeared on another Nickelodeon show, *You Can't Do That on Television*, and the Nickelodeon Kids' Choice Awards began pouring slime on celebrities too. Maybe it should have been called Slimelodeon instead?

papyrus

(*puh-PIE-ruhs*), noun

A type of paper made from the soaked and dried pulp of the papyrus plant, used by ancient Egyptians, Romans, and Greeks to write or paint.

The museum has scrolls of papyrus with ancient Egyptian hieroglyphics on them.

paraphernalia

(*par-uh-fuh-**NEYL**-yuh*), noun

Stuff you need for a specific activity.

The most important skydiving paraphernalia are parachutes.

Synonyms: accoutrements, gear

queue

(*kyoo*), noun or verb

1. *(noun)* A line you have to wait in.
2. *(verb)* To line up.

The queue for concert tickets wraps around the theater three times!

Riddle Me This

What's the only five-letter word in the English language that's also a letter of the alphabet? *(Psst, you were looking right at it!)*

sarcophagus

(*sahr-**KOF**-uh-guhs*), noun

An ancient stone coffin.

When archeologists found King Tut's tomb, they were afraid they would be cursed if they opened up his sarcophagus.

spittoon

(***SPIT**-teyk*), noun

Ever see an old western movie where the cowboys are chewing tobacco and spitting into a bowl? The bowl is a spittoon.

Don't knock over the spittoon, because Grandpa's tabacoo spit will spill out. (Ewww!)

squeegee

(*SKWEE-jee*), noun or verb

1. *(noun)* A tool with a piece of rubber that wipes water off a flat surface.
2. *(verb)* To use a squeegee.

Even if they aren't dirty, my sister loves to squeegee the car windows when we stop for gas.

Level Up!

The word *squeegee* has been around since about 1844. It's thought that it comes from an old nautical word, *squeege*, which means to press or squeeze. Some sources claim its first purpose was to clean a ship's deck, and in 1851, Herman Melville's *Moby-Dick* mentions a similar tool called a "squilgee."

talisman

(*TAL-is-muhn*), noun

A lucky charm. (But not the magically delicious cereal.)

Alfred's talisman is a medallion he won at the 5K race. He now wears it any time he wants good luck.

Zamboni

(*zam-BOH-nee*), proper noun

A small truck that scrapes and melts the top layer of ice at a rink, creating a new, smooth surface.

The Zamboni zips around the rink to quickly clean up the ice, so then the hockey team can zip around the rink.

zarf

(*zahrf*), noun

A sleeve slipped onto a handleless cup to use as a holder and protect your hand from heat.

When my mom buys a cup of coffee, she loves getting a cardboard zarf—otherwise she says her cup's too hot to handle!

THERE'S A WORD FOR THAT!

Words to describe the previously indescribable

Okay, as this book has shown you, apparently there's a word for everything. But...what if you don't know what to call something? Maybe you don't know what it is, or you simply forgot what it was called. Well, instead of simply saying "THAT THING OVER THERE," you can call it a *doohickey* or a *whatchamacallit* or many of the other—um, what do you call them? *Thingamabobs*? Oh!—the words in this section.

bric-a-brac

(**BRIK**-*uh-brak*), noun (singular or plural)
Random, small items that are only of value
to the person who collects them.
*My mom thinks my squishie collection nothing but bric-a-brac—but
each and every one of them represents something special to me!*
Synonyms: bauble, gewgaw, gimcrack, knickknack, tchotchke, trinket

doodad

(**DOO**-*dad*), noun
1.   A gadget or tool whose name you have forgotten.
2.   A small, pretty object used to decorate.
*Penelope's necklace comes with a small little doodad
that she can use as a key to open her jewelry box.*
Synonyms: doohickey, thingamabob, thingamajig,
whatchamacallit, whatsis

doohickey

(**DOO**-*hik-ee*), noun
Something that doesn't have a name...or it
does and you can't remember it.
*There's a doohickey I had on New Year's that spins around and makes
noise, but I can't remember what it's called. Oh yeah, it's a noisemaker!*
Synonyms: doodad, thingamabob, thingamajig,
whatchamacallit, whatsis

folderol

(**FALL**-der-all), noun

1. Nonsense talk or foolish ideas.
2. A knickknack or other small, worthless item.

My sister thinks the laundry can fold itself—what folderol!

thingamabob

(**THING**-uh-muh-bob), noun

Some gadget or gizmo that has a name you
don't know or can't remember.

My little sister calls my straightening iron a thingamabob
even though I told her its name a hundred times!

Synonyms: doodad, doohickey, thingamajig, whatchamacallit, whatsis

thingamajig

(**THING**-uh-muh-jig), noun

That thing that has a name—you know, that thing over there...

When I remembered the name of the thingamajig, I did a little happy jig.

Synonyms: doodad, doohickey, thingamabob,
whatchamacallit, whatsis

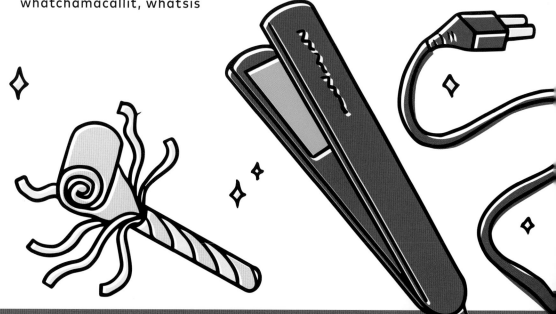

whatchamacallit

(*WUHCH-uh-muh-kawl-it*), noun
A thing that has a name you don't know or can't remember.
My brother lost his whatchamacallit, and I couldn't help look for it because I had no idea what thing he meant!
Synonyms: doodad, doohickey, thingamabob, thingamajig, whatsis

Pop Culture

When they created their newest candy bar in 1978, the chocolate wizards at Hershey really didn't know what to call it. Eventually, an executive at their advertising agency, Patricia Volk, decided to call it what it was: a Whatchamacallit! The Whatchamacallit is still being made today, although it can be difficult to find. The crunchy candy bar features peanut-butter-flavored puffed rice, topped with a layer of caramel, and coated in milk chocolate. Time for you to go whatchamaEATit!

```
<!DOCTYPE htr
<html lang="en">
<head>
<title> A WIDGE
```

whatsis

(**WUHTS**-*is*), noun

Same as a whatchamacallit
(but much shorter).

*I can't keep the names of the tools
in the woodshop straight, and
neither can my friend, so we call
the sharp, curved one a whatsis.*

Synonyms: doodad, doohickey,
thingamabob, thingamajig,
whatchamacallit

widget

(**WIJ**-*it*), noun

A small gadget, device,
or piece of software.

*Joe works in a factory where
he creates a bunch of random
widgets for people to fidget with.*

Synonyms: gadget, gizmo

Pop Culture

The word "widget" has wormed its way into the online world. A virtual widget is a cluster of code that can be pasted into a website, game, or app to create a new function. Bloggers use widgets to add social media videos and images to their pages, and Minecraft gamers use widgets to view all the players on a server. Widgets are easy to use because you just have to copy the code and paste it—you don't have to write the code yourself.

GINORMOUS WEBCAM

FROYO BOLLYWOOD

BRUNCH COSPLAY

PIXEL LABRADOODLE

JEGGINGS SPORK

HANGRY BROMANCE

GLAMPING SITCOM

CRASHWORDS!

The power to create your own fresh, new words

At the very beginning of this book, you learned that new words are added to the English language all the time. But did you know that *you* have the power to help create these new words? That's right, new words don't come from a bunch of word scientists brainstorming in a room—they are made by everyday individuals like you!

One way to create new words is by mixing already existing words together to create a new one. Like, if you went to a store full of monsters, you could call it a *monstore*. Get it? *Monster + store = monstore*. Or if you had a living robot, it'd be a *cyborg*. Because *cybernetic + organism = cyborg*.

These new words aren't the same as compound words, which take two words in their entirety and put them together to make one word. Examples of compound words are *starfish* or *treehouse*. With *starfish*, you don't lose any letters or sounds from the original words *star* and *fish*, right?

But with *monstore* and *cyborg*, parts of the two original words disappeared when they got smushed together. *Monster store* is a mouthful, but *monstore* is nice and smooth.

Remove some letters from *cybernetic* and *organism*, put them together and you make a shorter, snappier, and much easier-to-say word—*cyborg*!

So if *monstore* and *cyborg* aren't compound words, what do we call them?

Portmanteaux!

This may be the first time you've heard the word *portmanteau*, but you probably already know tons of them:

breakfast + lunch = **brunch**

brother + romance = **bromance**

Bombay + Hollywood = **Bollywood**

chill + relax = **chillax**

costume + play = **cosplay**

croissant + doughnut = **cronut**

electronic + mail = **email**

friend + enemy = **frenemy**

frozen + yogurt = **froyo**

gigantic + enormous = **ginormous**

glamorous + camping = **glamping**

hungry + angry = **hangry**

jeans + leggings = **jeggings**

Labrador + poodle = **Labradoodle**

motor + pedal = **moped**

picture + element = **pixel**

pug + beagle = **Puggle**

situation + comedy = **sitcom**

spoon + fork = **spork**

sports + broadcaster = **sportscaster**

stay + vacation = **staycation**

World Wide Web + camera = **webcam**

Portmanteau is a French word, though. And it's a little tough to say. Plus, it was invented so many years ago! It's time to create a simpler, cooler term in English. The words crash together, right? So, let's try:

CRASHWORD.

Perfect. With a vehicle crash, a car rarely remains in one piece—a bumper, mirror, or wheel might fall off and roll down the street. When words crash together, imagine some letters tumbling off the page. The letters that are left get smushed together.

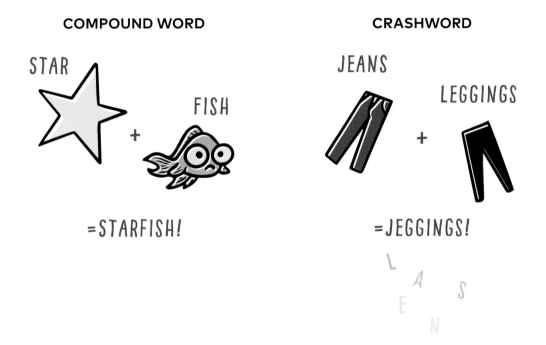

COMPOUND WORD

CRASHWORD

STAR
+ FISH
=STARFISH!

JEANS
+ LEGGINGS
=JEGGINGS!

Why don't you create some of your own CRASHWORDS?

When you see someone walking a cute puppy, you can call it *adogable* (*adorable + dog*).

If you have a half-day at school, pack yourself a *snunch* (*snack + lunch*).

When you have to take icky medicine, you might *gruzzle* (*grumpy + guzzle*) it.

When you take your photo in front of a bookshelf, it's a *shelfie* (*shelf + selfie*).

If your teenage brother is always playing video games, he's a *screen-ager* (*screen + teenager*).

See how it's done?

So go ahead, make up your own **CRASHWORDS**. And use them all the time. Maybe your friends will start using them, and then their friends will, and their friends too, and so on and so on...until, one day, you might see your very own **CRASHWORDS** in the dictionary!

Create Your Own Crashwords

Hints for getting started:

▶ Think about things that happen or emotions we have that have no words to describe them. What about when you make a mistake in a game but the result winds up being far better than your original plan? Did you ever cry from happiness, like after winning a championship or getting a puppy? There are no words to describe either of these things. What else in life NEEDS a word?

▶ Two words that mean the opposite can sometimes go together to mean something in the middle. That's how we got *frenemy* and *staycation*!

▶ Sometimes words that are long or complicated need a nickname. Just like Samantha can be Sam or Christopher is Chris, "situation comedy" is *sitcom,* and a "croissant doughnut" is a *cronut*.

▶ Look for words that have similar letters or sounds, like how the -*ster* in *monster* sounds a bit like *store* to make *monstore*.

The Master of Making Up Words

Author Roald Dahl was a master of the ~~portmanteau~~ *crashword*. In fact, the Oxford University Press published a dictionary of eight thousand made-up words that appeared first in his stories. (But not all are *crashwords*—some are *spoonerisms* and *malapropisms*.)

In Dahl's novel *Charlie and the Chocolate Factory*, he invents a plethora of portmanteaus to describe Willy Wonka's *scrumdiddlyumptious* candies.

scrumptious + diddly = **scrumdiddlyumptious**

Scrumptious means mouth-wateringly yummy, and in the novel *The BFG*, Dahl used *diddly* to mean different or unique. So Wonka's Scrumdiddlyumptious Bars were a deliciously rare chocolate candy!

Besides inventing extraordinary candies, Dahl is just as well known for creating dangerous beasts. A ghastly Dahl creature is the Red-Hot-Smoke-Belching Gruncher from *The Minpins*.

grind + cruncher = **gruncher**

Here's another example: In *James and the Giant Peach*, the Chief of Police mistakes Mrs. Spider for a gruesome beast called a Vermicious Knid. These creatures appear again in *Charlie and the Great Glass Elevator*. Where did Dahl get such a horrifying name? Perhaps he used one of these equations:

vermin + vicious OR *pernicious* = **vermicious**

Vermin are disgusting animals, pests like rats or cockroaches. *Vicious* means deliberately cruel or violent, and *pernicious* means something that can cause great harm or even death. YIKES!

(*Vermicious* is also a real word that means "wormlike," but since spiders aren't wormlike, and Dahl was known for being creative with words, we can assume he was making a crashword. Plus, *Knid* is definitely a word he made up, as there is no record of anyone but Dahl using it!)

Index

A

B

C